WHEN
YOU
PRESIDE

HOW TO PLAN AND
CONDUCT

Informal Round Table
  Discussions

Formal Business Meetings

Service Club Meetings

Panel Discussions

Symposiums and Forums

Conferences

Workshops

Business Conferences

Staff Meetings

SIDNEY S. SUTHERLAND
Chairman, Department of Agricultural Education
University of California, Davis

Preface

This book is written for my neighbor across the street and for all of the thousands of people like her in this country of ours; the men and women who are willing to step to the front and take the lead in community, civic, and business affairs. It is written to help the persons, who, like my neighbor, take the time and expend the effort to work for the good of their respective communities; the kind of people who are elected to lead women's clubs, service clubs, chambers of commerce, parent-teacher groups, and school boards; the kind of people who belong to and support those many groups which are working for the betterment of our way of life.

It is written, too, for other persons, who as a part of their jobs, must work effectively with people in groups; persons who supervise, lead, and direct; persons who must help the groups they lead to think through their problems, make decisions, and lay plans for constructive action.

In effect, it is written in two parts. The first three chapters discuss and describe general principles and practices which should be of interest to all, regardless of their leadership roles. The remaining chapters treat specific kinds of meetings, only a few of which may be of interest to you.

The ideas expressed in this book have come from many sources. Wherever possible, recognition has been given to the person or persons who have contributed them, not in footnote references, but in the script itself.

It has been written to you and for you. If it helps you in your leadership role; if it hits the mark more often than it misses, it will have been time and effort well spent. May it help you when you preside.

Sidney S. Sutherland

Acknowledgements

I wish to acknowledge my gratitude and my deep indebtedness to the following persons for the help which they have given:

1. To Wesley Smith of the California State Department of Education, Elwood Juergenson of the University of California at Davis, Gertrude Roskie of Montana State College, and my neighbor across the street for reading parts of the manuscript and for their many helpful suggestions.

2. To Paul Teetor, Editor-Manager of the ROTARIAN for permission to reproduce the drawings by Henry Wenclawski, and for furnishing photostatic copies of these drawings which were reproduced originally in the ROTARIAN.

3. To the secretaries of Kiwanis International, Rotary International, and Lions International for permission to quote from materials prepared by their respective organizations for the guidance of club presidents.

S. S. S.

Table of Contents

CHAPTER   PAGE

   I. So You're in Charge 1

  II. Kinds of People You Find in a Group 6

 III. Your Bag of Tricks 18

      1. How to get people acquainted 21
      2. How to use the buzz session 26
      3. How to present problems and how to lead
         group thinking 32
      4. How to use the brainstorming session 44
      5. How to get and keep people interested 50
      6. How to invite, introduce, and use a speaker 59
      7. How to make clear explanations 68
      8. How to present proposals involving change 73

  IV. Kinds of Meetings and Where to Use Them 79

   V. Leading Round Table Discussions 87

  VI. Conducting Formal Business Meetings 101

 VII. Presiding at Service Club Meetings 117

VIII. Conducting Panel Discussions 126

  IX. Conducting Symposiums and Forums 137

   X. Planning and Running Conferences 143

  XI. Planning and Conducting Workshops 159

 XII. Conducting Business Conferences and Staff
      Meetings 168

      Index 178

CHAPTER I

SO YOU'RE IN CHARGE

So they're holding a meeting! And you're in charge. Sooner or later it seems to happen to almost everyone— businessmen, housewives, mechanics, farmers, truck drivers, engineers, you, and me.

Maybe you brought it upon yourself. Perhaps there's a problem of management in your firm and you've called a conference of your associates to thresh it out. Maybe, like fame, you've earned it. Perhaps your neighbors have elected you to the city council and they in turn have selected you as chairman. Perhaps, (also like fame), you've had it thrust upon you. The phone rings and a feminine voice says, "The ladies of the Monday Club want to meet and discuss plans for raising money for the new community swimming pool, and WE WANT YOU TO LEAD THE DISCUSSION!"

America is not only sweet land of liberty. It is also the land of meetings. Meetings to discuss problems large and small; meetings to point with pride and to view with alarm; meetings to plan, meetings to review; big meetings, small meetings; formal gatherings and informal ones. And all of them need leaders to make them go.

Within the next day or the next week, the next year or the next few hours, the odds are all in favor of your being called upon to take the lead in one of them. For if you're the kind of a person who would be attracted by the title of this book and would take time to read it, you're the kind of a person who has already been tapped for such a job or likely will be soon. So perhaps you'd best read and study it now; when you're called upon to take the chair, it will be too late.

Let's assume that if this hasn't happened to you, it probably will. You find yourself in charge, looking at a lot of

1

expectant faces belonging to people just waiting for something to happen. It's all yours. What are you going to do about it?

For most of us, at least those of us who are not extreme extroverts and who are not automatically the life of every party, that dead silence, those expectant faces that greet one at the beginning of every meeting, is an appalling experience. It really starts the butterflies fluttering in our stomachs.

A Jewish boy, one Khaime Riskin, who had recently come to America from his newly formed country of Israel, summed it up neatly. Khaime went out to visit some high schools in this country to see how we did things over here. On his return, he reported to his fellow students at the University on his experiences: "You see hundreds of starink faces," Khaime said, "just sittink there and lookink at you. I'm tellink you, it's terrible!"

It needn't be terrible. It can be fun; fun for you and fun for the group you're leading. But how to do it so that it will be a pleasure and not an ordeal for you and your associates? You may read the rest of this book if you want to, and you should learn a lot about the finer points of conducting successful group meetings in general. That's why it has been written. But if you'll just read this one chapter and then put into practice the four things that are emphasized in the next few paragraphs, you will have the key to effective group leadership.

1. BECOME ONE OF THE GROUP AS QUICKLY AS POSSIBLE. You're already set apart from them physically by virtue of the fact that you're the leader. That blank silence is a wall between you and them, and between each individual in the group and his neighbor. Break it down! Get with them. Be informal and at ease. Forget yourself. Don't stand on your dignity; smile, and watch them relax. Become one of the group actually as well as in spirit. If they're sitting, sit with them. Move as close to them as possible. Get acquainted with them, and get them acquainted with each other. Become identified with them. Effective dem-

ocratic leadership of a group lies in relinquishing your status and so-called authority as leader as quickly as possible, and in getting the members of the group to take over this responsibility. That sounds like a paradox. Nevertheless, it is true. The quicker you can toss them the ball and have them grab it and run, the better you're functioning as a leader.

Get them relaxed, acquainted, and at ease; get them to take the initiative; become one of them.

2. GET THEM TALKING AND PARTICIPATING IMMEDIATELY. The surest way to throw a wet blanket on any group discussion large or small, is for the leader to attempt to start it off with a formal, prepared speech. It doesn't matter how well you do it or how important the things are that you feel impelled to get off your chest. The longer *you* talk, the tougher it will be to get them started talking and participating in the meeting.

It seems to be a natural impulse for a leader to want to talk, especially at the start of a meeting. But consider this for a moment. If you're going to do all or most of the talking, why call the meeting at all? Again, if you feel the urge to talk, how about them? Perhaps they like to hear themselves, too, the same as you do. So watch that impulse to make a speech, and smother it.

You want this meeting to be an interesting one. Then mark well and remember that participation begets interest; interest begets more participation; more participation begets more interest, which in turn . . . well, even the psychologists don't know which comes first, but they all know that interest is both a *cause* and an *effect* of participation. Like the old story of the hen and the egg, we don't know which comes first, but it doesn't matter. In the poultry business you can start with hens and get eggs. In a conference you can start with participation and get interest. It's just that simple, but many people who should know better, don't observe that rule, and run into unnecessary trouble.

If you talk longer than it takes to present to the group an interesting question or problem; if, as the meeting progresses, you find yourself talking more than fifty per cent of the time, watch out for danger signals. You aren't doing so well as a group leader. *You* may be interested, but are *they?*

3. GIVE THEM SOMETHING TO THINK ABOUT. Conducting a meeting and leading a group discussion is nothing more nor less than leading group thinking. If you want a group to think, they must be given something to think about. It takes a problem to start people to thinking. Groups do not discuss topics or subjects readily, but they will discuss problems. So either present a problem yourself to start the discussion or ask the members of the group to state the problem which they have met to talk over.

In presenting a problem state it briefly, clearly, succinctly, and *ask them what they are going to do about it.* Then keep still and let them solve it, helping them out only when they need it.

4. HELP THEM HELP THEMSELVES. Your major job as a leader is just this. You do so by relieving the tension at the start of a meeting through creating an informal atmosphere and becoming one of the group. You continue it by getting them to talk and to take part in the discussions. You foster it by giving them problems or by helping them select problems to solve. Finally, you make it possible for them to think these problems through by questioning, by encouraging the quiet ones to talk, by keeping the discussion from getting off the subject, and by making use of all of the know how, all of the good judgment, all of the sound reasoning that the fifteen or fifty members of this group represent.

Don't do their thinking for them. Help them to help themselves. You should be the *last* source of information—literally.

Remember these four things and practice them in conducting conferences, round-table discussions, formal meetings, panels—any kind of a meeting where you want group participation. They are the keys to successful group leadership.

1. BECOME ONE OF THE GROUP AS QUICKLY AS POSSIBLE.

2. GET THEM TO TALKING AND PARTICIPATING IMMEDIATELY.

3. GIVE THEM SOMETHING TO THINK ABOUT.

4. HELP THEM HELP THEMSELVES.

Of course there is more to it than this, and, of course, it isn't as simple as it may sound. However, as you read the succeeding chapters, notice how often these principles are the foundations of the tried and approved procedures of leading groups.

CHAPTER II

THE KINDS OF PEOPLE YOU FIND IN A GROUP

The most effective meetings are not just one-man shows. There is a tremendous amount of latent leadership in any group. It is a part of your job as a leader to recognize this leadership, to use it, to direct it into useful channels, and to get it working with you rather than against you. To do this you must first know how this leadership is expressed and the various forms it may take.

Just as "all the world's a stage, and all the men and women merely players," so each group has its cast of characters. Some are heroes, some are villains; some seek the spotlight, others avoid it; some have speaking parts, others manage the props. No one assigns these roles; each player assumes the one that fits his or her own personality.

Do you know someone who invariably is elected secretary of every organization to which he or she belongs? Probably you do, for there are many of these people. That is their method of expressing their urge to play a leadership role. They keep the written records of the matters discussed and of the decisions made. They are the unsung heroes of many successful organizations.

In contrast, do you happen to know some person who seems always to be "agin" everything? Unfortunately, you probably know one of these, too, for there seems to be one in almost every group. He's one of the villains, and (worse luck) not the only one.

So you'll have people in your meetings who naturally assume roles which are helpful. You'll also find others, but not so many who hinder, work against, and detract from the work of the group.

Dr. D. M. Hall in his book entitled "The Dynamics of Group Discussion," published by The Interstate, identifies

6

and describes at least fifteen roles which he states must be played by the members of any group in order to get effective group discussion and action. I'm sure you'll recognize them, and we've borrowed quite a bit of Dr. Hall's description in the following paragraphs.

Here they are:

1. *The Initiator.* He's the person who's always starting something—bringing up a new problem, suggesting a new activity, a new plan for the group to discuss. Generally the leader must play this role, but it's mighty nice to have several initiators in the group to help you out. He not only has the initiative and the imagination to sense problems, but also the ability to clarify, define, and state them so that they present a challenge to the other members.

2. *The Orientor.* The person who's likely to ask, "Now, just what is our problem? What is it we're trying to accomplish?" He helps focus the thinking and the talking of the group on the problem at hand, and serves to keep them on the right track. This is another role which the good leader must be prepared to play, but if you're lucky there's another "orientor" in the group you're leading.

3. *The Facilitator.* The person who keeps the pot boiling and the discussion going, generally by questions like, "Now, Bill, you said you were opposed to a door-to-door canvass to raise funds. Would you explain that?", or "Sam, I didn't get exactly what you were driving at in that statement; would you repeat it and make it a little clearer?" He's a kind of catalyst for a good discussion, and a couple of uninhibited facilitators in your group take a big load off your shoulders as a leader. Because, unless you've a facilitator or two in your conference, that's another role you must play.

4. *The Encourager.* The one who (though he may not enter the discussion actively himself) stimulates others to greater activity by showing approval, giving encouragement, etc. He smiles, nods his head, pantomimes a hand clap, or holds his hand up with his thumb and finger forming the well-known "ok" sign whenever someone makes a statement with which he agrees. Doesn't it give you a nice, warm feeling when you've made a statement and an enthusiastic "encourager" gives you the high sign that says, "You tell 'em. Them's my sentiments, too."? That's another role for the leader to play, but lest you get the idea that your job is getting complicated, there's just one more that is your responsibility if someone else doesn't take over.

5. *The Harmonizer.* The smoother-outer, the really mature person who, realizing that progress is based on differences of opinion, and that differences and arguments must

occur in any spirited discussion, makes a rational attempt to have all sides of the question considered. He often saves the day and reduces tension by a pointed and humorous story or quip. What a "harmonizer" Will Rogers would have been and was! Be thankful if you've a harmonizer in your group, and be prepared to be one if you haven't.

As indicated, these are parts which a leader must be prepared to play, but only as long as they are not taken over by other members of the group. For to be an effective leader is to relinquish leadership as others are able to assume it, and as soon as an initiator, an orientor, a facilitator, an encourager, or a harmonizer makes himself known by his contributions to the discussion, encourage him to take over this role and help him do so. For while the next roles to which we'll introduce you are not generally within the province of the leader, you might have to take some of these responsibilities, too.

6. *The Recorder.* The one who keeps a written record of the decisions and the actions of the group, and who reports them to the members of the group itself or to the public. The secretary who keeps the minutes of a formal meeting is the recorder. This is a very definite leadership role and an important one. As such, it is generally recognized and someone designated to perform this function officially as soon as a group is organized. It seems also to require an even more well-defined group of characteristics than most

other roles. Have you noticed how often a person who is elected or asked to serve as secretary of one organization is found to be serving in that same capacity for several others —in fact, almost every group to which he or she belongs?

7. *The Evaluator.* The person who tries to determine the progress which the group is making towards its objective or objectives. This is the one who, when the discussion seems bogged down or going around in circles, is likely to speak up and say, "Well, we don't seem to be getting anywhere this way; let's see whether this other tack will help." Or, when things are going well, "We seem to have pretty well decided that such and such is the thing to do." This role is closely related to and perhaps often combined with—

8. *The Analyzer.* The one who takes notes and perhaps even records the extent to which each member of the group is participating and contributing to the solution of the problem under discussion. Further, he may analyze the progress of the group as a whole, the way in which it is cooperating or failing to cooperate in working toward a common objective, as well as the effectiveness of the leader in directing and guiding the group. Often the analyzer is the third member of a team consisting of the leader, the recorder, and the evaluator-analyzer, each of whom has such a well-defined part to play, that it is officially recognized and designated.

9. *The Summarizer.* The person who brings together ideas which have been contributed by other members, points out their relationships to each other, and suggests a course of action. A friend of mine who is a confirmed "meeting goer," as a member of the board of regents of a midwestern university and active in numerous business, civic, and social organizations, has this to say of the summarizer:

"If I could pick my role in a meeting, that's the guy I'd want to be! I know lots of them and I envy them their ability to kinda lean back after everyone has had his say and come up with something like this, 'Now, Bill gave us a lot of good facts about the need for equipment in the Boy Scout cabin, and I agree with what Tom said about wanting our troop to be the best in the district. I can't go along with Al entirely when he says this is the worst troop in town, but I do agree that it isn't the best by a long way. So why don't we just, each of us, contribute five bucks apiece and ask the other dads to do the same and buy 'em the equipment they need.' When he says that, all the rest begin to nod their heads in agreement and the whole thing is settled right there. Yep, if I could have my choice, I'd want to be a summarizer."

That's what a summarizer does. He takes what Bill and Tom and Al have said, boils it down to its essentials, and suggests an appropriate action. It's a real leadership role,

and every group needs one. Furthermore, this is a part which the leader should not play. If he has to take over this duty, as sometimes happens, the group isn't functioning as it should.

10. *The Expeditor.* The person who is primarily concerned with the comfort of the individual members, the physical setting, and the materials of the meeting. He is the one who distributes paper and pencils when there is

writing to do; he finds a chair for the late comer, opens a window, and adjusts the shades if the room be too close or the sun shines in someone's eyes. Generally a kindly, bustling, officious (but not offensively so) person who takes satisfaction in the material and the physical items which make a meeting go as it should. He's easy to identify. Watch for him in the next meeting which you attend.

11. *The Fact-Seeker.* The Indians would call him "Man who wants more facts." Whenever a problem is under discussion he is the one who comes up with the statement, "I don't believe we have enough data on which to make a decision. I'd like a few more facts before I decide." He is generally a p r e t t y straight thinker, and his role is important since, in the heat of discussion, opinons are apt to be more freely given and considered than are the basic facts of the case. He calls attention to the importance of paying attention to the realities of the situation and helps in that way to arrive at a sound decision.

12. *The Fact-Giver.* The one who cites from his own experience or from authority, facts which bear upon the problem under consideration. If the subject under discussion is the raising of the school tax, he is the one who gives the tax rates for all the other districts in the county, compares them to the local rate, and calls attention to whether the local tax is too high or too low. Since facts are necessary, his contribution and the importance of his role cannot be underestimated.

13. *The Status-Giver.* The person who is invited and encouraged to become a member of the group because his accomplishments, his position, his attitudes, and his abilities are known and respected not only by members of the group, but by the general public. We generally notice status-givers operating in larger groups. Having the president of the university, the mayor of the town, or the big boss greet the assembly, welcome them to Miami or Boston or Los Angeles (especially Los Angeles) is practically as essential and as standard in opening any large convention meeting as is the registration desk.

14. *The Compromiser.* The person who is willing to give ground, to admit that there may be two sides to the argument, and who relinquishes his stand in order that progress may be made. Like the harmonizer, it takes a really adult and mature person in every respect to play the compromiser role and to appreciate its import in group processes.

These are the more important, if not all, of the desirable roles in group processes. However, as we hinted at the beginning of this chapter, not all of the roles which will emerge when people gather together to thresh out common problems *are* desirable. The roles described above are primarily *democratic* roles—normal reactions of persons working together for a common objective. In contrast to these, we have certain *autocratic,* and dominative roles emerging; roles which are primarily selfish.

Dr. Hall identifies eight of the selfish or dominative roles. Watch for them as you get acquainted with them. They are the ones who will cause you trouble as a leader and at least a measure of annoyance as a working member of a group.

1. *The Playboy.* Appears in many guises. Sometimes he brings the morning paper with him and busily peruses the sport page, commenting on the progress of the Los Angeles Dodgers while the leader is trying to get the meeting under way. Ridicules everything. Writes notes or makes sketches which he passes to his neighbors. Tries to draw attention to himself and to show his lack of interest in the objective of the group by horseplay or cynicism; refuses to do his part and tries to prevent others from doing theirs.

Dr. Hall calls him a "dodger." In his least obnoxious stage he merely goes to sleep and snores.

2. *The Aggressor.* The tough guy. As a boy, this individual was the mean little kid who featured the sneer and the threat "I'll get you after school" in order to maintain his leadership. He's grown up now but still tries to control by fear. He ridicules, questions, and attacks the status of others in the group. From "I'll get you after school," he has graduated to "What do *you* know about it, anyway? You're crazy!"

3. *The Monopolizer.* The gabby character who starts out to ask a simple question and prefaces it with a five-thousand word statement that wanders all over the map and has little or nothing to do with the problem under discussion. Can be counted upon to speak up at every opportunity, even interrupting others to do it, and to ramble on and on ad nauseum and ad infinitum. Makes ten words do the work of one. The uninhibited extrovert who just loves to hear himself talk and indulges his passion. A close relative to the—

4. *Recognition-Seeker.* Mr. Know-it-all, who knows all the answers, knows all the important people who know all the answers which he doesn't; has done everything and done it well. Knows how to run the government; how to conduct the war. The present day version of "Me und Gott," who now says, "Me and the Governor are just like that." Expects and demands special consideration for all of his statements and positions, and shows it by the manner in which he makes his pronouncements.

5. *The Blocker.* The person who is "agin things"—everything. Usually has no good reason for his negative attitude, but invariably opposes everything that the majority of the m e m b e r s favor. (I don't like blockers!)

6. *The Wool-Gatherer.* The person who is congenitally unable to keep his mind on the subject under discussion or to think consecutively for more than two or three minutes. Just when everyone else is enthusiastically discussing ways and means of raising funds for the community swimming pool, he pops up with a question or statement regarding the mating habits of the head hunters in Borneo or some other subject equally remote.

7. *The Whisperer.* Probably a sub-species of the playboy or the recognition-seeker whose specialty is starting a whispering conference with his immediate neighbors to the confusion of the leader and the discomfort of the rest of the group. Rarely, if ever, contributes to the group as a whole.

8. *Mr. Zipper - Mouth.* He just won't talk. Sits like a bump on a log. Listens, doesn't disturb anyone, but doesn't contribute. Probably just shy—certainly inarticulate.

These are some, perhaps not all, unfortunately, of the bad ones. We hope they won't be in your group, but if they are, be prepared to deal with them. You will find some helps in Chapter V.

Several of these leadership roles are important enough so that they long have been recognized. The initiator-harmonizer-orientor-facilitator acts as the *leader* of the group. The recorder is the secretary who keeps the written records of the deliberations. These you know and are familiar with.

The trend, however, is to expand this team to four instead of two. Quite often a member may be particularly well informed on the subject under discussion and his facts may be needed by the group in order to reach a sound conclusion. Such a person may be invited to take part because of his wider knowledge. Thus the role of "fact-giver" may be expanded into that of the *consultant* who supplies facts and acts as a third member of a team. Sometimes he is called a "resource-person."

Groups may not always proceed in a straight line toward their objective. Sometimes they may tend to wander down inviting by-ways instead. Sometimes, in spite of the efforts of the leader, all do not participate. Therefore the role of "evaluator" and "analyzer" is often combined and a fourth member joins the leader, the recorder, and the consultant. He is called an *observer*. He analyzes and evaluates progress.

The functions of each of these will be described more thoroughly in later chapters, but the modern leadership team now comprises four—a *leader*, a *recorder*, a *consultant*, and an *observer*.

CHAPTER III

YOUR BAG OF TRICKS

Regardless of the kind of meeting you may be called upon to lead, there are some general techniques and devices which you should be able to use if and when necessary. Perhaps we should not call them "tricks." They are not tricks in the sense that you are trying to confuse or baffle, but rather special kinks or methods to help you accomplish your main objectives as a leader.

The best meetings are informal. Just as you probably have a better time at a masquerade ball where everyone dresses up in silly costumes and lets his or her hair down literally and figuratively, than you do at a formal dance or an afternoon tea, so do people react better when meetings are less formal. You can't be informal in a group of strangers. Therefore, the first skill you will need is in *getting your members acquainted with each other.*

Good meetings, from the point of view of both leader and member, are those which are interesting. Interest is such a potent factor in determining what we do and how we do it that perhaps the greatest gift you could be given as a leader is skill in *getting* and *keeping people interested.*

Thinking is the forerunner of effective action. Really democratic leadership consists of helping people define, state, think through, and solve their problems. As a leader, you have to be an initiator, at least sometimes. On you falls the responsibility of getting this thinking process started and of guiding and directing it. Thus your third skill should be that of *presenting problems and leading group thinking.*

19

When a problem or a job is too large to tackle as a whole, it is just good sense to break it down into smaller parts each of which presents a smaller, easier task. Similarly, the larger a group becomes, the more difficult it is to handle—as a single group. To get the benefits of full participation by all, the logical thing to do is to break that larger group into several smaller ones. This you can do by learning the many uses of the *buzz session*.

Many meetings, especially the larger ones, make use of a speaker. When it becomes your responsibility to *arrange* for, *introduce,* and fit that *speaker* into your programs, it is obviously satisfying to be able to do that well.

So, we present to you these and other skills to add to your bag of tricks and to help make your meetings better and more effective.

HOW TO GET PEOPLE ACQUAINTED

Before people will discuss or work together on a common problem and do it effectively, they m u s t know each other. Furthermore, they must be relaxed and at ease. Have you ever noticed a group of people just before a meeting, a PTA meeting or a Public Schools Week program or some other affair? As they wait for it to begin, there is a buzz of conversation. Everybody is talking to everybody else. They're gathered in groups discussing the weather, Mrs. Smith's new dress, the income tax, the local basketball team's chances of winning the league championship, all sorts of topics. Then someone indicates that the meeting is about to start. The groups break up. They take their seats. And now what happens? Dead silence. Everybody is waiting for someone to break the ice.

Even in a small group this is likely to happen, and the larger the group, and the less well acquainted each one is with everyone else, the deeper and more profound the silence.

As a leader of any small discussion group, your first job is to get each person relaxed, to get all acquainted with each other, and in the mood to talk. There are a number of ways to do this, but regardless of which one you use, there are two good general rules to follow.

1. *Introduce yourself first, and do it in the way in which you wish them to introduce themselves.* People in groups are peculiar in that they want a leader to follow, and they want a pattern set for them. It's your job to set the pattern. If you

would like to know not only the names of the members but their connection with and their interest in the problem under discussion, give your name and describe briefly your contacts and interests, and then ask them to do the same.

2. *Let them hear the sound of their own voices just as soon as possible* on something they can say easily and well.

Among tried and effective ways of getting people acquainted with each other in discussion-sized groups are the following:

Introduce them yourself. If you know them all, and the group is small, this is the quickest, probably the most used, but certainly the least effective way. It won't get them to talking, it won't put them at ease, and you can't possibly introduce any member of even a small group as well as he could do it himself. You don't know much about him to begin with, and you're not as interested in him, either. So the next logical method is—

Let each one introduce himself. After you break the ice by introducing yourself and telling a little about yourself in terms of your interest in the subject of the meeting, ask each one in turn to stand, give his or her name and do the same. That works well for a small group. Stress first names and nicknames. No one can be bothered in a really good discussion with the more formal modes of address. When you introduce yourself, say, "I'm Sadie Smith," not "I'm Mrs. Alfred E. Smith," and request that the rest do the same.

So, with a small group a good lead-in might sound something like this:

"The first thing we want to do here this evening is to get acquainted or at least better acquainted with each other. Let's introduce ourselves. I'll start it off, and after I've introduced me, you introduce you. And tonight, let's forget being Mister or Miss or Mrs. Introduce yourself by the name you like to be called or by the name your friends call you—either your first name or your nickname, or both, because that's the way we're going to address you in this meeting. I'm Betty Brown. My interest in discussing this school lunch program lies in the fact that I've got three school-age children who generally lunch at school at least once a week. Now, starting over here, will each of you give us your names—first names, please—and tell us briefly of your special interest in this topic."

This will get your meetings off to a good start, for you will be accomplishing these things:

1. You'll know, if you listen, the names of your group members and get a clue as to their attitudes toward the problem or topic.

2. You've got every one of them to say something within the first few moments of the meeting.

3. You've got each one relaxed and at ease because he's spoken right up in meeting and said something, and the next time it will be easier because the ice is broken.

4. You've made it easy for each member to become identified with the group and to feel secure because you've asked him to talk about something that he's more interested in and knows more about than anyone else—himself.

5. You've set the stage for the informality that makes for free discussion by stressing first names rather than formal titles.

This is a good method and a widely used one, but so widely used that sometimes it is well to vary it and—

Have each one introduce himself, and then see how well they remember the names of the others. Try it this way. Start out just as though you were going to have each one introduce himself. Let the first five or six introduce themselves, tell their little stories, and sit down. When you get to about the seventh, ask him to introduce not only himself, but to reintroduce the five or six people who preceded him. If he can't do it, let the rest of the group help him out. A note of caution. If No. 7 is obviously a shy, retiring individual, skip him. He'll hate you if you don't. Then continue individual introductions for three or four more and then pick on the next one to introduce *all* of those preceding him. Continue this until the last person in the ring has the job of introducing not only himself, but the entire group. This will really get people acquainted and break the ice.

Another variation and one which works well with small groups is to:

Have each one introduce his neighbor. This will work whether the group is seated around a table, in a circle, or in rows. Simply announce that you will ask each person to introduce the one on his left, and give them a moment or two to introduce themselves and to get the information that they need for the introduction. Better specify the kind of information you wish given so as to keep them under control. Then pick a starting place, either at the end of the row or at some break in the circle, and select the person to start the introductions. Before long each one will be trying to outdo the other in presenting his neighbor to the group.

Still another variation, and one that works especially well where many of the group are total strangers to each other, is to—

Use place cards. This works so well that it should be almost standard operating procedure where the conference group is seated around a table or tables.

In this method, you have everyone introduce himself; you still stress first names and nicknames, but you have each one write out his own name plate or place card and leave it in front of him where everyone can refer to it during the meeting.

All this takes is a supply of pencils and enough 5 x 8 inch cards to supply one to each member. As you open the meeting, state again that you want them to get acquainted, and that since it is easy to forget names, you want them to make their own place cards. You set the pattern by folding your own card in the middle so that it forms a tent with each roof 4 x 5 inches. Then print your first name in large capital letters and your last name in smaller capital letters below it, and set it on the table in front of you so that all can see it. Better yet, print your name on both sides. When you have done this, have the rest make out their name plates and set them on the table.

When they have all finished, introduce yourself verbally as in the preceding methods, and have each member of the group in turn make his little presentation.

With this device, not only do first names become the standard mode of address immediately, but the cards will be referred to time and again by members and yourself when names are forgotten.

Caution. Don't destroy these place cards if you're going to be meeting again with this group. They'll ask for them at the second meeting, and you'll be embarrassed if you don't have them.

So here are five ways, four of them good, of getting acquainted. Use them, and experience will teach you other and perhaps more effective methods or variations of these which you can use to break the ice, put people at ease, and get them talking. Just remember and judge every method by the following standard. Just as the general said that the way to win wars was to get there fustest with the mostest; the way to start a good discussion is to get the mostest people talking the quickest.

HOW TO USE THE BUZZ SESSION

One of the best ways of getting the maximum participation in a large group is by means of the buzz session. You'll appreciate how it got its name the first time you see and hear it in operation. The buzz session takes a very natural impulse and puts it to good use. When you have been at a large dinner, say fifteen or twenty people, have you ever attempted to keep a conversation going with everyone taking part? Pretty difficult, isn't it? The natural tendency is for you to talk to your partner on your right, the one on your left, and the one or two directly across the table from you. Therefore, instead of a general conversation involving all those present, if left to your own devices, you'll break up into conversational groups of five or six. These are natural buzz sessions.

In a formal meeting when a slate of candidates is presented and you are asked to vote, isn't your natural tendency to turn to your neighbor and talk it over with him first? Now you wouldn't stand up in meeting and discuss the candidates with everyone, but you'd have no inhibitions whatever about talking it over with your nearest seatmates.

It seems that in a group of any size, just the sheer weight of numbers keeps the most of us from expressing ourselves freely. Only the most uninhibited seem to be entirely free from this fear of the group and have the courage (or the brass) to speak up. The rest of us would rather keep our thoughts to ourselves. Just where the dividing line is where a group becomes something that puts pressure upon us and keeps us mute is difficult to measure. Ordinarily a group of six or eight doesn't have this effect and in a group of this size we speak up unafraid. When it grows to twelve or fifteen, the pressure begins to make itself felt, and the larger the group the less we like to speak up.

The buzz session takes advantage of the fact that we will talk and discuss freely, even the most reticent of us, in a group of five or six; but that we just won't talk in a group of fifty or sixty with the same freedom.

On page 140 is a picture which shows a large group which the chairman or leader has divided up into buzz sessions. The picture was not posed. It was taken during a symposium in a statewide meeting of young farmers. A speaker had just concluded a short, prepared talk and the buzz session groups of five or six persons each were busily discussing what he had said and were deciding on the questions they would ask him in the discussion period to follow.

The chairman had briefed the audience on the procedure to be followed, and had divided them up into groups before introducing any of the speakers. The directions he gave them went something like this:

"After each speaker finishes, we're going to give you exactly two minutes to talk it over and decide what questions you want to ask him in the discussion period to follow. In order to do this, we're going to divide you into groups of six. After each speaker has finished, I'll give you a signal. When I do, the first three people on my right here on the front row turn around and face the three directly back of you; the next three do the same, and so on. In the third row, divide yourselves up into threes the same way, and *you* turn and face the three back of you; the fifth, seventh, ninth, and all odd numbered rows do the same. Now, let's have a rehearsal. All in the odd numbered rows turn around and face those in the even numbered rows. All right. Now, we'll call each group of six a "buzz session" group. When each speaker finishes and I give you the signal, do just as you did now. Elect or decide on a chairman for your little group any way you see fit. Then talk it over and do two things—decide on the questions you want to ask him and *who* should do the asking."

In the picture, they are really buzzing, and enough questions came out of these sessions to keep the speakers busy answering questions for two hours after they had finished their set speeches.

The buzz session, then, is just a period when a larger group or audience is divided into smaller groups, generally six people to a group. They should face each other. This is easy in an auditorium or any formal seating arrangement where they are seated in rows. Just have odd numbered rows turn around and face those in the even rows. Have them elect or decide on a leader to guide the discussion and someone to act as spokesman for the group later. Then just let them talk, and stop them when they begin to run down. Better put a definite time limit on them or they'll keep going indefinitely. Sometimes, instead of buzz session groups they are called "six by sixes," six people discussing for six minutes.

If you will stop and think for a moment, you will realize that this is merely taking advantage of the most natural kind of a reaction. After a speaker is finished, your natural tendency is to turn to your wife or your husband or your companion and make some comment or ask his or her reaction. The buzz session just systematizes this tendency and puts it to work.

How and Where to Use It

Perhaps the most effective use of this device is in symposiums and forums where one or more speakers deliver set talks which are to be followed by questions or comments from the floor. If used in a symposium, time should be taken for a short buzz session after each speaker, and paper and pencils provided for each group so that they may record their questions and have them when the question period arrives. It is amazing how much the audience participation is stepped up, and how much more intelligent questions and comments are forthcoming. Neither is there any danger of encountering one of those devastating blank silences which greets the moderator when, after the speaker finishes, he asks expectantly, "Now, are there any questions?" For instead of hopefully and fearfully addressing his query to the audience as a whole, the leader can start things off, if necessary, by pointing to any buzz group and asking, "What is the question *your* group wishes to ask the speaker?"

Where the buzz session is not used, audience participation in forums and symposiums is quite apt to be limited to the few who: (a) love the limelight, whether they have anything to contribute or not, (b) want to show off their knowledge of the subject by taking issue with the speaker, (c) feel impelled to ask questions to make the speaker feel that he was appreciated, or, (d) just for the heck of it. As a result, the caliber of the questions asked is quite likely to be sub par.

In contrast, the buzz technique gives each person a chance to talk it over with five of his peers. Questions which might be asked are evaluated and discussed and the obviously silly or trite ones discarded. As a result, questions are good and (a comforting thought for the moderator) forthcoming.

This procedure works equally well following panel discussions, and a longer period may well be allotted to the single buzz session than in a symposium where there should be sessions after each speaker. Two minutes after each symposium speaker, and from five to six minutes following a single speaker or a panel, should be about the right length for buzzing.

In smaller, round-table discussion groups, its use and effectiveness is somewhat limited. Since the group is smaller, the need for dividing it into still smaller segments is less, and the seating arrangement does not lend itself too well to this sort of a division. In larger groups, however, it has been found to be effective when the group has tackled a rather large problem, and after discussing it for awhile, seems to bog down. The procedure here would be for the leader to divide them into sixes, restate the problem, and let them buzz for five minutes or so. It has been found that after this break and the informal discussion that results, the answer that seemed so obscure when the entire group was groping for it, would emerge from one of the smaller groups.

Whether or not it would work in the more formal atmosphere of the business conference is problematical. There seems to be no good reason why it should not.

Other Specialized Uses

In Workshop Conferences. The buzz session has been used very effectively in workshop conferences in at least two ways:

1. To provide questions and problems to be assigned to conference sections.

2. In considering reports of sections to the general assembly.

In the former, the chairman of the meeting of the opening session of the workshop might announce that there would be three sections, each of which would discuss problems in a certain general area. He would then announce the subject of the first section, ask the buzz session groups to consider and suggest questions and problems that the section might undertake to answer, and put them to work. At the end of a minute or two, he would call them to order, ask for their suggestions, and record them or have them recorded so that the leader of that section would go into his section meeting armed with a set of problems to present. Two more buzz sessions and each of the three sections would have their work cut out for them.

More effective yet, is the use of the buzz sessions in the closing general sessions of the workshop conference when the committees or sections come back to report to the general assembly. You are all too familiar with what usually happens when a committee makes its report to the larger assembly. The secretary of the committee either reads his report or distributes mimeographed copies to the assembly. When it is presented, he moves its adoption, someone seconds his motion, and without too much consideration, the assembly adopts it. As a result, anyone who has ever edited reports of this kind can recount weird tales of the strange statements that are sometimes swallowed and adopted. This is just too uninteresting a procedure to bring out the consideration and discussion of these reports which they merit.

Here is where the buzz session works beautifully. After the report is presented and the motion is made and seconded to adopt it, have it considered in a five-minute buzz session before voting on it. It is surprising how quickly and easily errors, inconsistencies, omissions, etc., will be detected by these smaller groups which would have gone unnoticed if considered in the usual manner.

In formal business meetings, when a really difficult problem is under consideration, use may also be made of the buzz session. Breaking up into small groups for an informal discussion often brings forth sound proposals and immediate action. A complete discussion of this procedure is given in Chapter VI.

As more experience is gained with this relatively new device, it is probable that more effective uses will be found. It is well worth a trial in many situations where discussion in a larger group bogs down.

NO. 3

HOW TO PRESENT PROBLEMS AND HOW TO LEAD GROUP THINKING

Presenting Problems

There are at least four acceptable methods of getting a problem before a group for consideration, discussion, and action:

1. For the leader to formulate and state the problem.

2. To have an individual in the group describe an actual problem situation.

3. To have the group select it by means of a problem check list.

4. To have the problem presented by having it acted out by the members—role playing.

Which method you will use will, of course, be determined by the subject under discussion, the makeup of your group, and the conditions under which you are conducting the meeting. All are good and all have their place.

Presenting the Problem Yourself

This is probably the most common method, and perhaps the easiest to use. In stating a problem yourself, state it clearly, definitely, briefly, and as interestingly as possible. Present it as a question, not as a topic or as a statement. Always see that the statement itself calls for an answer. A problem is a difficulty; a situation which calls for thinking for its solution. It may be stated as an actual case which calls for action, or as a general statement of conditions calling for a more general conclusion. A problem which describes an actual case or situation is generally more interest-

32

ing and more easily solved than one that deals in generalities. For example, answering the question "How can we overcome the shortage of qualified help?" may be of interest to a group of employers, but an actual case brings it much closer to home and admits of a more definite solution.

Having Someone in the Group Present the Problem

Suppose, for example, the group had met to discuss the general problem of a shortage of qualified help. Someone early in the discussion says, "Well, take my situation, . . ." That's just the opportunity you should be waiting for. Call him immediately to the front of the room, get him to describe his problem, and then use the following procedure in conducting the discussion.

It consists of using a blackboard "pattern" and leading the group to the solution by directing them through the seven steps of good thinking. It is a particularly good device where there exists an actual problem situation.

The blackboard pattern used looks like this:

JUST WHAT DOES HE WANT TO ACCOMPLISH?

1._____

2._____

Important Facts	Possible Courses of Action
1.	1.
2.	2.
3.	3.
4.	4.
5.	
6.	Solution
7.	
8.	
9.	
10.	
11.	

It is best to have a team—a *leader* for the discussion and a recorder to write on the blackboard or wall chart the contributions of the group. So, with a recorder to assist him, the leader should then:

1. *Ask one or more members of the group* to describe the situation clearly and briefly.

2. *Help the group to limit and define* by deciding on the most desirable outcome of this situation. Have the recorder put it on the blackboard. Use questions like, "What is the best thing that could happen in this situation?", "What do we want to have happen?"

3. *Get inferences and opinions* by asking, "Now that you know the situation and what we want to happen, what would *you* do?"

   There may be one or two hardy souls who will stick their necks out and volunteer an opinion. If so, have the recorder list them on the board under "Possible Courses of Action" and have him write after each solution the initials of the person offering it.

   If there are no courses of action forthcoming, then,

4. *Get the important facts.* Ask, "In your opinion, what are the really important facts in this situation that should influence our decision?" Have the recorder list them, abbreviating and briefing them as much as possible.

   As contributions are made by members of the group, get common agreement that the fact given *is* important.

5. *Ask for revisions of courses of action* suggested (if any) and other possible courses of action. Have the recorder list and initial those given.

6. *Help the group to weigh facts and decide.* Take each "course of action" listed in turn and ask three questions as follows:

   a. (To the contributor) "What facts listed support your conclusion? What facts are in conflict?"

   b. (To the group) "If we did this, would it accomplish what we want to have happen?"

c. (To the person who described or brought up the problem) "Could you *do* this?" If any one fails to measure up to the standards implied by these questions, have it erased.

After all suggested courses of action have been so tested,

7. *Ask the group for its conclusion.* Ask for the course of action or combination of courses of action remaining that seems the best. If they are unable to reach a conclusion as a group, break up into a buzz session. Give them two or three minutes to discuss the possible courses of action and to decide on the best. Then call for reports from each buzz group. It is surprising how much agreement there will be and how quickly a conclusion is reached.

8. *Suggest that the action agreed upon* by the group be tried out and that the results, good or bad, be reported later to the group.

With the guidance of an alert leader, this device really keeps the thinking of the group focused on the problem under consideration. This is a "guided" discussion; almost a "directed" one, but notice that the leader never indicates, or even implies to the group *what* to think, but only *how*. So, even though closely directed, it is entirely democratic.

Whether this method, with its formalized, rather rigid pattern, is used in a conference discussion or not, it is still an excellent guide as to the course that a discussion should take in the solution of any problem. For groups are made up of individuals. As individuals think, so do groups. And the way to solve a problem is to use good thinking procedure. The steps listed at the end of this chapter are the processes which a group as well as an individual goes through in working its way out of a difficulty. Not only do they constitute the thought process that we generally use, but fortunately they are the steps in *good thinking*. See that your group follows them.

Using a Problem Check List

A problem check list is just a listing of the more common difficulties which the leader feels the group may have encountered and therefore may wish to discuss. The example on page 37, entitled "Some Pressing Problems in Wholesale Credit" was prepared to open a meeting of credit managers.

The purpose of such a check list is to furnish the members of the group with suggestions as to problems which might be troubling them, and from which they could choose the one or ones to discuss.

To use this device, have a sufficient number of these lists duplicated so that each member may have a copy. Distribute them as the meeting opens, and ask each member to check with a pen or pencil the ones he has met recently. When you see that they have finished, read the list aloud, pausing after each problem to find out how many had checked it. Mark on your copy the ones most often checked. When you have gone through the list in this manner, you will find four or five which the group consider most important. Then simply ask which one of this smaller, selected group they wish to discuss first and start the discussion.

This device is one of the best ways of getting the meeting under way where only the general subject and not the specific problems have been set beforehand. Note that it gets all members doing something immediately—a sure-fire technique.

In preparing such a check list, take your cue from the example given. Notice that the difficulties listed are general in statement and scope. You may not be a credit manager yourself, but the odds are you'd find some things you'd check, too.

SOME PRESSING PROBLEMS IN
WHOLESALE CREDIT[1]

Do you ever have to handle any of these?

1. Underfinanced businesses (lack of working capital).
2. Overexpansion of retailers.
3. Taxes.
4. Inexperienced retailers.
5. Shortage of qualified help.
6. Scarcities of merchandise.
7. High prices.
8. Competitive selling—using credit to expand sales.
9. Rising cost of inventories.
10. Diminishing returns and expanding overhead.
11. Pending government controls.
12. Inadequate information on financial statements.
13. Lack of coordination.
    a. Salesmen and credit.
    b. Credit and sales force.
14. Lack of adequate accounting by retailers.
15. Poor follow up on past due accounts.
16. Request to return merchandise.
17. Requests for extension of terms.
18. Too free extension of credit.
19. Scare selling.
20. Lack of information on credit reports—both newcomers and old accounts.
21. Dishonest accounts.
22. Keeping credit files current.

Have It Acted Out—Use Role-Playing

This technique draws its value from the fact that many problems, especially those involving relationships between people, are not easily put into words. Words, furthermore, are not easy to remember. A dramatic or striking scene on the other hand, may never be forgotten.

---

[1] Courtesy of Dr. William R. Blackler, formerly Chief, Bureau of Business Education, California.

This is not a new device, having been introduced in this country in 1927, by an Austrian, J. L. Moreno. It simply calls for the unrehearsed acting out of a problem by members of a group, so that it may be better understood and visualized by the group. Closely allied to role-playing is the psycho-drama or socio-drama, the latter differing from role-playing in that the actors are briefed and rehearsed in their roles.

Role-playing is attracting increasing attention as a classroom device for children as well as a dramatic method of presenting certain kinds of problem situations to adult groups.

In one of its most effective forms, it may develop out of a problem being *described* by the leader or a group member.

The essential elements are these:
1. The problem must involve people whose attitudes, opinions, and feelings can be defined.
2. The acting and the actors are unrehearsed.
3. The action should last only a short time—five to ten minutes—as long as it remains spontaneous.
4. There is no script; the action and the lines develop as the scene progresses.

An actual use to which this device was put may serve to clarify just what it involves. A group of teachers at an institute meeting were discussing some of their problems. One came up with this: "Sometimes I want to get my students excused from other classes so we can make field studies of interesting events and situations. Quite often these opportunities come up without much advance notice, and I have to go to my principal, say at 9 o'clock in the morning, and try to get permission to take them on a field trip that very day. How can I do this and still keep peace in the family?" The leader suggested that he describe an actual situation, and that two members be selected to act it out. Questioning brought out the characteristics of the principal, his attitudes, and his general reactions to requests of this kind. The situation selected was an actual one. A program had been arranged in a neighboring town where representatives of leading co-operative marketing associations were staging an "Information, Please" meeting. They, as a panel, were available to answer questions on cooperative markets put them by junior and senior students from nearby high schools. The teacher had to approach his principal the next morning to ask permission to have a group of students excused from classes the rest of the day to attend and take part in it.

The group selected one man to play the part of the principal, who seated himself behind a desk at the front of the room. Another one was drafted to be the teacher. He walked up to the front of the room, greeted his fellow actor, and the show was on.

At first there were a few snickers and wisecracks from the audience, but in less than no time, they were all attention as the teacher made his pitch to get his boys released from classes, and the principal raised objections. After not more than three minutes or so, the leader told them to cut the action, and the discussion really got under way.

Three minutes of seeing it acted out gave these teachers more tips on what to do and what not to do in a similar situation than thirty minutes of just talk.

There seems to be two phases or parts to presenting a problem through role-playing, prior to the subsequent discussion.

1. *A "warming-up" process* in which the problem is stated, the characters in the drama are drawn, the stage is set, and the actors chosen. This should be done by the group, not by the leader alone.

2. *The actual role-playing* where the actors, drawn from the group, give their unrehearsed version of the situation.

The discussion which follows analyzes the action, the roles, and draws conclusions on how to handle this and similar situations.

The potential uses of this device are many. It is particularly valuable in training people for public service and public contact jobs, teachers, salesmen, receptionists, clerks, waitresses—a whole host of jobs. It is a real help in solving human relations problems of all kinds, as it portrays so well actions, expressions, feelings, and attitudes that cannot easily be described.

Leading Group Thinking

Leading a group discussion is really helping people to think through one or more problems and to arrive at a solution, a conclusion, or a decision. Therefore, it is important that you as a leader know *how* people *think*. What goes on between one's collar and the part of his hair from the time a person senses a problem until he solves it? Let's review how we think as individuals in order that we may know how we think in groups.

The Way We Think	*An Example*
1. We face a problem or difficulty.	1. Shall I trade in the old bus on a new car or run it another year or two?
2. We limit, define, and clarify the problem.	2. Our car is eight years old and has nearly one hundred thousand miles on the speedometer. It still runs pretty well, but the motor is noisy and the body is full of squeaks and rattles. Every time I ride in a new car I want to kick mine right in the rear tire. The paint is okay but dingy; the upholstery on the front seat has a hole in it. We'd have to arrange with the bank to pay for a new car on installments, but if we get a good trade-in, I guess we could manage it.
3. We form an opinion, a tentative conclusion, a guess as to the probable answer to our problem.	3. I believe I'll trade it in on a new car if I get a decent trade-in allowance on the old one.
4. We find facts to back up our opinion or oppose it.	4. I take my car downtown and talk to the Ford dealer. He looks it over and offers me what he calls the "Blue Book" value. It isn't as much as I expected. He takes me for a ride in a new Ford. Gee, it's a nice car; it even smells good. I talk to Bill Good, my neighbor, who just traded his old car in on a new one. He says, "Yeah, they're

nice, all right, but you have to wash, polish, and clean it up every week. With the old crate, I just let it stay dirty. The new one uses lots of gas, too. They can't seem to get the carburetor adjusted right." I talk to my friend, Pete, who is a mechanic. Pete says he doesn't know whether he'd do it or not. He says repairs on a car that old come fast and high. I stop in at the bank and they say they'd finance the deal if I decided to buy.

5. We weigh the facts and change our opinion on the basis of the facts.

5. I talk it over with the wife. We both want a new car. We're tired of the old one. Most of our neighbors have new cars. Ethel says she's ashamed to drive it downtown and afraid to take it on a trip out in the country. On the other hand, they won't give us much for our old one and the payments will run us pretty short on our budget. The old car would do for another year and maybe we could save enough so we could pay for it easier. We haven't had any trouble with the old car lately. It uses a little oil, but runs all right. My wife finds an article in the morning paper that says car production may be cut drastically and new cars may be hard to get next year.

6. We reach a conclusion based on all available facts.

6. I decide to see the dealer once more and if he'll up the trade-in on my old car by fifty dollars, I'll buy a new one.

7. We act on our conclusion.

7. He increased the trade-in allowance, and I drove the new car home today.

This illustrates our mental processes when we tackle a problem calling for a *decision;* a choice between two or more courses of action. We think in much the same way and go through the same steps in the solution of almost any problem.

Since a group must be led through these steps in thinking through and discussing their problems, it is important that you as a leader of a group know them and know them well.

Again, these steps are:

1. Recognize a problem or difficulty.
2. Define, limit, and clarify the problem or situation.
3. Form an opinion or inference as to its solution.
4. Get the facts.
5. Weigh the facts and revise opinions if the facts make such a course necessary.
6. Reach a conclusion or solution based on all available facts.
7. Take the action indicated by the conclusion.

* * * * *

Just so you will be prepared for it when it happens, be advised that not all individuals nor all groups think straight all of the time. Quite often they may fail to follow these steps or otherwise are guilty of loose thinking. Some of the most common errors are these:

1. They fail to define and clarify the problem.
2. They start looking for facts without first forming a tentative conclusion or inference.
3. They stop in their thinking at Step No. 3. They form an opinion and refuse to find or recognize facts in weighing this opinion. They "jump to conclusions" and omit Steps No. 4, 5, and 6 entirely.
4. As a result of bias or prejudice, they refuse to weigh the facts correctly and revise their opinions.
5. They seem unable to reach a conclusion even when all the facts are in and have been carefully weighed.
6. They fail to act on their conclusions—to follow through.

Therefore, in leading a group in the solution and discussion of a problem, see that they follow the recognized steps in good thinking and help them avoid the common pitfalls of loose thinking.

To do this:

1. Present the problem clearly, briefly, and interestingly.
2. Ask for answers, for opinions, without supporting reasons. Try to get all possible answers.
3. Call for reasons from the minority group first, then from the others.
4. Select the answer that has the most popular support. Call for reasons for and against.
5. When all such reasons and facts have been given, lead the group to a decision based on these facts.

HOW TO USE THE BRAINSTORMING SESSION

Someone has said, "A man's judgment is no better than his facts." In the same vein, it might be said that the thinking of an individual or a group can be no better than the number of inferences, tentative solutions and new ideas that can be developed as possible solutions to a given problem. There is no doubt that many individuals and many groups often fail to arrive at a satisfactory solution to a difficulty simply because all possible alternatives are not brought to light and given the consideration which they deserve.

It has been facetiously said that in any group or any organization for every "idea man" there are twenty "what's the idea" men. In other words, for every one of us who can think constructively, and who can come up with new ideas, there are many others who think negatively and devote most of their time thinking up reasons why a particular thing can't be done.

As a result, many large business firms have recently begun making use of the "brainstorming session" in bringing to light ideas not only for solving administrative problems, but for developing new sales methods, new products, and new uses for products. Among these are such corporations as U. S. Steel, Ethyl Corporation, General Motors, Hotpoint, U. S. Rubber and many others. The creator of this process is Alec F. Osborn, a co-founder of the Batten, Barton, Dursten and Osborn advertising agency. Many years ago, Mr. Osborn began using small groups of employees to brainstorm such things as slogans and new products, and a few years ago organized brainstorming as a regular service for all of his firm's clients.

The essential features of a brainstorming session are few and simple.

1. The number of participants is not material but should be large enough so that there are potentially many sources of ideas. Brainstorming groups may be anywhere from 10 to perhaps 20 or 25 in number.

2. The participants should be of somewhat equal status so that all will feel free to contribute their ideas. They should also have some familiarity with the problem.

3. They should be seated around a table facing each other so that the groundwork for free discussion is laid.

4. Arrangements should be made for one or two secretaries to be present to take down ideas as fast as they are presented. In smaller groups, a tape recorder or dictaphone may also be used to record discussion.

5. The leader states the problem and also makes clear that certain ground rules are to be rigidly observed as follows:

   (a) Every idea presented must be positive.

   (b) There will be no comments allowed regarding any idea presented. Criticisms of ideas presented are absolutely barred.

   (c) Everyone is encouraged to speak up and to express ideas regardless of how crackpot or fantastic they may seem.

   (d) Members are encouraged to present ideas as rapidly as they come to mind, and the only limit on speed is the ability of the secretaries to record the suggestions made.

   (e) Members are also encouraged to "hitch-hike," which means to add to or revise ideas suggested by other members of the brainstorming team.

This technique is strikingly successful. In a recent session participated in by the author, a group of some 30 participants generated 154 ideas for the solution of a knotty administrative problem. Not all of these ideas were work-able, of course, and many of them were ordinary, run of the mill, unimaginative solutions which had been tried with only moderate success. Also, included in the list were many fantastic suggestions which were obviously unwork-able. However, out of the chaff of crackpot and routine suggestions came three or four which showed real promise.

Surprisingly enough, one of the most striking outcomes of this session is the way in which a seemingly fantastic idea stimulates someone else to build upon it and change it slightly so that it actually proves of value.

After the brainstorming session it is essential of course that someone evaluate, condense, and bring together the ideas presented, to discard those which obviously are not workable and to terminate the period with a listing of those which are worthy of further consideration.

This technique may be used in the solution of all sorts of problems. As an illustration of how a seemingly fantas-tic idea may develop into a usable one, a recent brain-storming session conducted by the extension service in California devoted itself to the problem of utilizing grazing lands where there was inadequate water for the livestock competing with the wild animals which normally graze on this area.

The grazing land under consideration was a forested or semi-forested area containing some trees and large shrubs. It was reported that someone in this group, knowing that during hot weather trees and shrubs give off a great deal of moisture into the air through their leaves, came up with the idea of placing plastic envelopes over the trees. The envelopes were to be fitted with channels which would collect the moisture given off by these plants and conduct it into receptacles at the foot of the tree. Thus, a certain amount of water would be collected for the use of livestock and wild animals. Now the typical "Doubting Thomas" would probably point out that while trees certainly do give off water, the amount would hardly be sufficient. Furthermore the cost of these plastic envelopes, which would have to be manufactured especially for this, would be prohibitive; also that covering the tree for an extended period of time would doubtless kill it; in fact, perhaps any number of reasons could be given why such an idea would be patently absurd. However, this suggestion did go to the evaluating committee, and on the committee were some men with imagination and of an inquiring turn of mind. As a result, they tried out this idea on a tree, and found to their surprise that in not too long a time they collected twenty-five gallons of water. The final result was the origin of at least a possible way of putting to use hundreds and perhaps thousands of acres of land now rendered unusable by virtue of lack of drinking water. Other equally fantastic stories have been reported as to the value of these brainstorming sessions in developing new ideas.

It will be seen from this description that brainstorming is creative thinking carried on as a group process which separates positive from negative thinking and generation of ideas from evaluation of their worth.

Brainstorming sessions should not be too long. The leader should be alert to note when the flow of ideas begins to slow down and to be ready with some plan to start them coming again. Some leaders set a limit of three minutes and at the end of that time have the brainstormers take a break, stand up, walk around, have a smoke, and discuss anything except the problem. After a few minutes they go back to their discussion again. It seems more logical, however, to play it by ear, and if at the end of the set time the session is still rolling in high gear, delay the break until it slows down.

Brainstorming Sessions for Larger Groups

The key to handling larger groups in brainstorming sessions is to make use of the "buzz session" technique and to break them up into smaller groups. Perhaps the optimum

number for a group which will operate as a single unit is
12-15. When the group is larger than that, use the procedure described below.

1. Divide the participants into groups of 6-8 persons.
Ask each group to seat themselves in a compact circle, and
to select a leader and a recorder. Give each recorder a
pencil and a packet of 6x8 inch cards on which to keep
a listing of the ideas generated by his buzz group. Ask each
group to select a name for itself such as "Braintrusters,"
"Aces," "MG's-Mental Giants," "MR's-Mentally Re-
tarded,"—any name which comes to mind. Record names
on chart or blackboard.

2. Put them through a warm-up session. A good device is
to use a picture or cartoon, and to ask them to name it or
give it a title. Introduce some competition by challenging
each group to come up with the largest number of names in
three minutes. At the end of that time stop them and ask
each recorder to count up the number of names his group
had generated. List on the chart the number brainstormed by
each group—the Aces, MR's and all the rest. Add the totals
and call attention to the large number of titles developed
by the entire group. It is not improbable that each group
would have found 15-20 names.

3. Have a short evaluation session to emphasize the
separation of generation from passing judgment. Ask each
group to take two minutes to decide on the best one or
two titles in their list. After they have decided, have the
recorders present their selections. Then, if you wish, have
the entire group try to pick out the one or two of the best.

4. Present another warm-up problem and go through the
same procedure as was followed in the first one. A problem
which is familiar to all should be used, such as, "How can
we keep our roadsides free from empty beer cans?" or
"How can we improve men's clothing—make it more comfortable and attractive?"

5. Present the main problem to be brainstormed following the same general plan as you used for the two warm-

up problems, except that more time should be given to the generation process. Try to maintain competition between the groups and continually challenge them to beat their competitors.

6. The evaluation process may be the same as was used in the introductory problems or the cards gathered from the recorders and turned over to a smaller group to evaluate at their leisure.

Summarizing, the conduct of this kind of meeting is very simple. The leader must be sure that the ground rules are understood; that the problem is stated; that those present are conditioned to present ideas; that the session be kept a free-wheeling, fast-moving succession of ideas, regardless of how foolish; that no one criticizes or comments; that all ideas are accepted as stated or as improved upon by a subsequent speaker; that a record is kept of all; and that, finally, the suggestions made in this session are evaluated and the grain separated from the chaff.

HOW TO GET AND KEEP PEOPLE INTERESTED

The highest praise that can be given to any meeting is, "That was *really* interesting!" The most damning criticism —"Gosh, what a bore!" Interest is the fountain head of attention and action. It is what starts us to thinking and keeps us alert. We think only about the things which interest us. We refuse to think about the ones that don't. It's the catalyst of group action.

How can we make our meetings interesting? How can we get and keep members of a group interested? The leader who puts into action the answers to these questions will be making a tremendous stride toward achieving effective group leadership.

There are at least two important facts that anyone who would seek to control or arouse the interest of a group should realize:

1. Interest is like a fire. It is much easier to get started and to keep going than it is to rekindle after it has gone out. So get your group interested at once, and try to keep them that way.

2. Even though man is supposed to control his actions by reason—to be a reasoning being—he is actually a creature of impulse. Impulses exercise more control over our actions and our interests than reason.

Therefore, we often are not at all interested in the things we ought to be interested in and that reason tells us we should be interested in. Instead, our interests are mainly governed by a number of natural impulses.

In the following paragraphs are described a number of procedures to use in making meetings interesting. At the same time the reason *why* these procedures arouse interest will be given. Notice how many are based on natural impulses that all people possess.

Techniques to Get and Keep Interest

1. *Get and keep everyone participating.* Jimmy Durante's plaint, "Everybody wants to get into da act!" is not just a gag. It's true. They do want to get into the act. So get your group members into the act as soon as possible. Keep your introductory remarks short—eliminate them entirely if you can. Use problem check lists to let them identify the problems they wish to discuss. Let them feel that they are taking important roles, that the meeting is theirs. People like to be doing something—to obey that activity impulse. Let them.

2. *Show your own interest.* A dead pan may be an asset in a poker game or a business deal, but not in a chairman or a group leader. When someone in the group speaks give him your undivided attention. Look at him and listen to him. Don't gaze out of the window or fiddle with your notes. Your actions speak louder than your words. Don't tell them how interested you are. Show it. Interest is infectious. It spreads. If you indicate by your manner that the subject really is vital to you and that you feel it is equally vital to them, they'll gradually take the same attitude. As soon as a few of the leaders in the group catch the spirit, it will infect the others.

This works in reverse, too. If you're bored or indifferent or act that way, expect the same reaction from them. People in groups have a strong tendency to imitate and to think and feel alike. Call it mob psychology or what you will, but recognize it and make it work for you, not against you.

3. *Identify and call on the interested members first.* Just as your interest in the subject will infect others, so will the contagion spread from one member to another. So as you start your meeting, watch for those who seem to have caught the spark and direct questions to them. Then as others begin to wake up, you can bring them into the discussion. This

isn't the time to call on the quiet guy over in the far corner. Save him for attention until you've got the others interested.

4. *Use humor.* This doesn't mean that you have to be a Red Skelton or a Bob Hope. It doesn't even mean that you have to be able to tell a funny story. As a matter of fact, if you're the kind of a person, (and most of us are), who just can't tell a story and make it really funny, avoid it like you would the plague. There's nothing unfunnier than an alleged funny story.

However, you'll find some wits in almost any group. Laugh at their wisecracks and encourage others to do the same. Often some catch phrase or a slip of the tongue can bring out the grins and the chuckles better than a planned gag or story. In a meeting recently, a member solemnly declared, "We should leave no stern untoned to get this job done!" The group had a fine time "untoning sterns" for the remainder of that meeting, but really got a job done.

Nothing seems to draw a group together and develop a "we" spirit like a good laugh. So plan to go along with whatever gag crops up. Smile and laugh with them and give them a chance to smile and laugh with you. To illustrate, a workshop was being held during the last weeks of a hot, muggy July. The first day everyone appeared fully attired with coats and neckties. The announcement was therefore made at the first meeting that thereafter coats and ties were taboo; that this was a work session and that they were to come dressed for action, not display. As luck would have it, the second day brought the leader a luncheon meeting that called for something more formal than a sport shirt, and the one o'clock general assembly of the workshop found him in violation of his own taboo. To the demands "Take it off; take it off!" the offending tie was removed, but a plan was born. Selecting the worst tie in his collection, the next morning's meeting found him apparently in willful violation of the no-tie rule, and a two-time offender. And this time it brought action. A delegation found a sharp pocket knife, advanced to the platform, and proceeded to prune his necktie just below the knot. Then they solemnly tacked it to the bulletin board as Exhibit A and returned to their seats. That did it! After that, laughs just generated themselves; everyone forgot his inhibitions and went to work.

The fact that the Danny Thomases, the Jack Bennys, the George Burnses and Gracie Allens and other humorists have the big radio audiences, should be tip-off enough that there's an inherent appeal to humor. Use it.

5. *Make everyone feel important.* Everyone likes approval; most everyone likes the spotlight; all like a sense of accomplishment. Take advantage of this. Show approval. When someone makes a contribution that is worth while, compliment him, especially the person who doesn't have much to say.

My neighbor across the street, among many other activities, teaches folk dancing. The other night she had a group of beginners "do-se-do-ing" in the multi-purpose room of the grammar school. As they rather awkwardly finished a set, she turned off the record player and told them, "You're wonderful! You really did that beautifully!" And did they feel good! Do we love approbation? We eat it up! So be an encourager and satisfy that need that we all have for a pat on the back.

Give everyone a chance to be in the spotlight. When you know someone who has had experiences to merit it, say, "Bill, you're pretty close to this problem and know more about it than the rest of us, what do you think about it?" Give Bill and Sue and all the rest their turn to shine, and watch them expand and their interest grow. Remember, the parties that were the most fun and which stick in your memory were the ones where *you* were the center of attention. The ones that bored you were the ones where you were the wallflower. It's just the same in a meeting.

When the group has thought through a problem well and has come up with a good solution, call their attention to it. As you summarize, highlight the fact that progress is being made, that they're accomplishing something. Nothing is more frustrating than lack of progress, so when you do get progress, emphasize it.

These three, love of approval, of prominence, of progress, are strong drives for interest. Be on the lookout for ways to use them. Often when you could operate alone as a leader, designating and using a recorder, a consultant, and an observer is worth-while just to share the stage with three others and to give them prominence.

6. *Arouse their curiosity.* There's hardly a stronger impulse in most of us than curiosity. Notice the reaction in any meeting when a late-comer opens the door. Everyone turns as if operated by a check line to see who it is. A fire siren brings everyone to the window or out of doors to see where the fire engines are headed. Now how can we use this? The story is told of Will Rogers in his early days in vaudeville. Each evening he came out on the stage in cowboy regalia and a lariat rope. Each evening he fiddled with the rope and started a few stunts as he wisecracked and commented on the foibles and follies of the day. The audience waited for him to do his tricks, but each time the curtain came down with no rope tricks done. His only purpose for the rope was to keep them curious and interested.

When you ask a question, never or rarely name the person first and then state the question. Instead, ask the question of no one in particular—*pause,* look around the room, and then designate the respondent. The pause gets everyone on his toes, curious as to whom it is directed. This device is valuable for other purposes, too. It promotes thinking by everyone; it builds up suspense, another good interest factor; it provides a change of pace.

Run the numbers ahead when recording on a chart or blackboard. Suppose at a PTA meeting the discussion centers around "What can we do to help improve our schools?" The leader has put the question to the group and one suggestion has been forthcoming. The blackboard or chart might look like this:

What can we do to help improve our schools?
1. Visit and confer with teachers in class.
2.
3.
4.
5.
6.

The five blanks immediately brings to each member the thought, "Well, there must be at least five more. I wonder what they are?"

Use a "strip tease" in displaying and talking from charts. Cover the message on the chart or graph with strips of paper fastened at the ends with thumb tacks or scotch tape. Pull off the strips to uncover each part as you discuss it, so that the group sees only what you have talked about and are talking about, and is left to wonder what you're going to uncover next.

7. *Keep a controversial discussion balanced.* Closely allied in some ways to curiosity, suspense is another strong interest factor. This is what keeps us up sometimes until 3 o'clock in the morning reading a detective story. We can't stop until we find out who killed the butler.

In formal business meetings, conducted according to the rules of parliamentary procedure, it is the duty of the presiding officer to see to it that following a speaker favoring the motion under consideration there should be a speaker opposing it. This, of course, is primarily to make sure that both sides have a fair hearing. However, this practice has another outcome, and when you preside make every effort to follow it. Recognizing and giving the floor first to the proponents and then to the opponents of a proposal keeps the issue in doubt—doubt builds suspense, and suspense builds interest. Similarly in an informal discussion, try to identify those who favor various sides of the problem under consideration. Then bring them into the discussion in rotation so that both or all sides are kept from piling up a preponderance of favorable evidence. Help the proponents of the less popular side by suggestions and leading questions, and keep from showing which side you favor. As long as you can maintain a reasonable balance in the arguments pro and con, so long will you have interest and suspense. Just as soon as the issue is decided, that interest dies.

8. *Keep your meeting free from distracting influences.* It's pretty difficult to keep your attention on two things at once. Uncomfortable chairs, too much heat or too little, noises from outside the meeting room, all serve to distract attention from the subject at hand. Be at your meeting place ahead of time and see that your meeting place is as free as possible from these upsetting influences.

Many leaders lay themselves wide open to another type of divided attention by passing out copies of printed, mimeographed, or other kinds of reading matter, and then trying to continue a discussion. *Don't ever do this! If the material is important enough to merit such action, stop the discussion right now and let them read it.* If it doesn't need to be read immediately, distribute it *after* the discussion. Nothing can be more futile (nor less interesting) than to ask a group to listen, discuss, and read at the same time.

How you dress can be a distracting influence, too, both to you and to your group. In your desire to make a good appearance, *don't dress up!* Go well groomed, yes, but wear your second best outfit, one in which you'll be and look comfortable and at ease. Then, too, you don't want to focus the attention of the group on you more than is really necessary. A too bright tie, an obviously new suit or dress can distract their attention just about as badly as a fire siren. Perhaps it is worse, for the siren stops eventually, and that red tie with the purple and green stripes stays as long as you do.

9. *Keep things moving and change the pace.* The leader of a discussion meeting has to play by ear; perhaps it is more fitting to say that he has to *conduct* by ear. He has to sense when things begin to drag and to speed up the tempo; he has to get the feel of correct timing and to see that it is maintained. No amount of pre-planning will accomplish this. It

will help, but often the group refuses to follow the script you have so carefully prepared. Some monopolizer will get wound up and seem to have no terminal facilities whatever. Mr. Wool-gatherer may have been day-dreaming just when the issue is being decided and have to have it explained again especially for him. You may have to get downright rude and interrupt your gabby member. You may have to keep your eye on the dreamer and get him involved in the discussion so it won't have to be rehashed for his benefit. Whatever you can do to keep things moving and to keep time from being wasted is worth doing. People like to see their meetings move; to get somewhere. They soon lose interest if they drag.

One specific thing which you can do to keep things moving is to watch your own timing. When you have a comment to make, make it snappy and make it brief. Don't fall into the habit of repeating and rewording contributions made by members. If they don't say it exactly the way you would, ask them if they mean thus and so, or accept it as stated. Don't try to put your words into their mouths.

Almost as bad as too slow a pace is to maintain the same tempo and the same routine all of the time. Again you'll have to play it by ear and to sense when a change is needed. If they've been debating an issue for some time and getting nowhere, break in and summarize the discussion, bringing out the points which have been made for and against the proposal, or call on your observer to analyze and sum up. Vary your procedure in presenting problems. Introduce role-playing where it can be done. Don't always use a blackboard to record progress; try chart paper or simply have the recorder keep the notes at her seat. Break up into buzz groups when the problem gets too knotty for the group as a whole to solve. The interest span of an adult group is longer than that of children or teen-agers, but it, too, has a breaking point. See, if you can, that it isn't reached.

In Summary. If you can make your meetings interesting, you've made a big step toward making them worth-while.

While getting and keeping people interested is more nearly an art than an exact science, do these things; practice until you can do them smoothly, and you'll generally get results.

1. Get everybody into the act just as soon as you can.
2. Be interested yourself and look it.
3. Don't be afraid of chuckles and laughs. Go along with the gag.
4. Share the spotlight; make everyone feel important.
5. Play on their curiosity.
6. Keep the arguments balanced; maintain suspense.
7. Watch the tempo.

HOW TO INVITE, INTRODUCE, AND
USE A SPEAKER

THE SPEAKER

The telephone rings at 1:15 p.m. Saturday afternoon and a voice over the wire says, "We'd like you to talk to our Rotary Club next Monday noon and tell us all about your recent trip to England. We meet in the Masonic Hall. Can you make it?"

The man who has been honored with the invitation to tell of his sojourn across the Atlantic isn't up on his mental toes so soon after lunch and answers, "Sure, I'll be there."

Click goes the phone at the other end, and the deed is done. The odds are that the Millville Rotary Club won't vote *that* talk the program of the year.

Let's consider the speaker first. He's really behind the proverbial 8 ball, whether he realizes it or not. Why? Well, here's what he's up against. What's he going to talk about? If he describes his whole trip and shows the colored slides which he has so carefully prepared for just such an occasion, it would take about two hours. How long should the talk be? What about the audience? Have any of them been to England? What are they interested in? art? business? climate? the old buildings? the effect of the buzz bombs? what? Where's the Masonic Hall? How do I get there? Whom do I ask for at the door? Should I be there at 12 sharp, 11:45, or 12:15? Who else is going to talk? Am I the whole program? Will they want to ask questions? Should I allow time for that?

Add to all the things he should know and doesn't in order to give an effective talk the fact that he has practically no time left to prepare for it, and what's the answer? Probably a frustrated speaker and a bored audience.

So, when you're arranging for a speaker, do the following:

1. Contact him personally by phone or by letter at least two weeks in advance; longer if he is a really important person and may have other engagements. In any event, give him time to prepare.

2. Tell him specifically what you want him to talk about, and *give his speech a title*. "The Reaction of the British People to Socialism," or "The English Businessman," not "tell us about your trip to England." Not only will a title give the speaker a lead and make his job easier, but it will also protect the audience from a vague rambling such as, "We left New York Harbor on Monday and arrived in Blackpool, etc., etc."

Just giving an interesting title to a talk can add that little extra fillip of interest that makes the difference between a drab performance and a sparkling one. Consider these titles —"I May Be Wrong!", "Some of the Swans *Are* Swans," "It Can Happen Here!", "An Immoral Victory," "That Inspiring Task." Don't they arouse your curiosity and make you want to hear what the speaker is going to say? So give his speech a title.

3. Give him some information about his audience—the number to be present, their interests, their ages, the walks of life they represent. He'll want to fit his remarks to his listeners; give him a chance to do so.

4. Give him the date, time, and place of the meeting, how to get there, who will meet and introduce him. A speaker who doesn't know these things and is worrying about them while driving or riding to his appointment is hardly going to be in tip-top fettle for a sparkling address.

5. Tell him exactly how long he is to talk and how much time to allow for questions.

6. Give him the names of the other speakers, their topics, and his place on the program.

7. Supply any other pertinent information about the room, the acoustics, facilities for projectors, etc.

Now he's in a position to prepare and give a talk to fit the occasion and his audience.

To make sure that he doesn't forget, and to make doubly certain that he understands, *confirm* your invitation and his acceptance *by letter*.

So the next time it falls to your lot to arrange for a speaker, do the things that have been outlined above, and both your speaker and your audience will bless you. Since it is probably easier to remember three or four things than seven or eight, probably the most important rules in inviting a speaker are these:

1. Invite him long enough in advance so that he has time to prepare.
2. Give his talk a title.
3. Tell him who will meet him and will be responsible for introducing him.
4. Confirm your invitation and his acceptance by letter.

Introducing a Speaker

There are probably more crimes committed by amateur MC's in making introductions than in any other of the many things that take place in meetings.

Perhaps the classic of classics is the one that allegedly was given the president of one of our better known universities. The president had received a letter from one of his former students asking in effect if one of the professors could be obtained as a speaker and naming the subject. Recognizing the name of the writer and being interested in the subject, the president himself accepted the invitation. Overawed by the prestige of his speaker, the jittery alumnus started his introduction thus:

"Ladies and Gentlemen. We could have done with a poorer speaker than the one we got for tonight. In fact, we tried to get a worse one but we couldn't!"

Some day some high-browed scientist is going to find out

why it is that when there are only two ways of doing even a simple job the inexperienced person almost invariably chooses the wrong one. Perhaps it's the same thing that makes a piece of bread always fall butter-side down. In any event, introducing a speaker is so easy when done right that there is no excuse for doing it any other way.

Let's take a look first at what you should be trying to accomplish. First of all, you're selling him to the audience; selling him and what he has to say. Next, you are starting a process that every good speaker will continue the minute he starts to talk. You are getting his listeners interested and directing their attention to the speaker and his subject. Finally, you are not only introducing him to the audience but also the audience to him, creating the kind of an atmosphere that will make the speaker want to put out and putting the listeners at ease and making them receptive. You are paving the way for him and making his road easier. You are not making a speech yourself; you are presenting the one who will do that job.

We said in the beginning that launching a speaker was so easy that there was no excuse for doing it in any other than the right way. Here's the proof. You only have to remember and to do these things:

1. Just before you introduce him, tell him in words of one syllable just how long he is to talk.

2. Tell the audience briefly what the subject is and why the speaker is qualified to talk about it. Tell what he has done that enables him to speak with authority, his title or position, his experience. Don't give his complete biography, but hit the high spots.

3. Pronounce the speaker's name only once and then as the final word of your introduction.

4. Lead the applause, and remain standing and looking at him until he has taken his place on the platform and is ready to begin.

5. Then, and only then, sit down and congratulate yourself on a job correctly done.

You might almost say that a good chairman or toastmaster is a man of four "Be's"—

1. Be brief.
2. Be sincere.
3. Be enthusiastic.
4. Be seated.

Let us analyze the five things which you should do in preparing the way for a speaker so that you will know why you are doing them as well as what to do.

All speakers seem either to talk far too long or not long enough. That's why it is absolutely essential that you impress on them just before they start that there is a time limit. Perhaps it would be well to show him your watch and say, "Look, it's just 8:35 right now. It will be not later than 8:40 when you take the floor. These people expect you to talk exactly one hour, and we want to be out of here at 9:45." That may sound pretty curt and you may be afraid of hurting his feelings by being so insistent on setting up terminal facilities for him. However, the most awful thing that can happen to you as chairman is to have to sit through the final half hour of the rambling remarks of a speaker who has long ago worn out his welcome, and watch the audience squirming in their seats, looking at their watches, and exhibiting all too well symptoms of utter boredom, while the speaker drones on and on and on. So save your fingernails and your ulcers by making as certain as you can that this doesn't happen to you. He should know and appreciate that the brain can absorb only what the seat can endure and cooperate with you.

Two objectives should be uppermost in your mind in telling the audience about the speaker and his subject: (1) to sell him and his subject to his listeners, and (2) to create suspense. In selling him, be sincere but not sloppy. Emphasize what he has done, the position he holds, his importance as a person and as a public figure, the experience he has had in the field of his talk. The more important a man he is in his own right, the less you need to tell about him and the less you should tell. The perfect introduction for the man in the White House, then, would be, "Ladies and Gentlemen, The President of the United States." That is sufficient. More would be utterly superfluous and out of place.

Tell about the subject first and the speaker later. The sequence should be: first the subject, next the man, finally his name. This serves as a natural build up to create suspense. By describing the speaker, the position he holds, his qualifications for speaking on the subject without indicating who he is or giving his name, suspense is automatically created, and suspense builds interest.

The formality or lack of it in your manner in making introductions will depend upon the occasion, how well you are acquainted with the speaker, and his prestige. A middle ground is the safest. Ponderous dignity regardless of the occasion is just as bad as launching the speaker by making him the butt of a joke. Humor is always good if it suits the occasion and if you can really use it effectively. Avoid it like the plague if you can't. Nothing can be quite as flat as an allegedly funny story that doesn't jell. If you can tell stories well, and you know that the speaker is one who is alert enough to top you and take advantage of it, a joke on the speaker, well told, is a natural.

There may be occasions when it is permissible to mention the speaker's name before its logical place—your final and climactic word, but they are so few that you would do well to forget them. Just consider these two examples and contrast them in terms of the suspense and interest each would create.

"Ladies and Gentlemen: We are fortunate to have with us today Dr. Melville Jones, noted authority on archeology, who is going to speak to us on the subject of 'The Cliff Dwellers of the Southwest.' Dr. Jones, as curator of the National Museum, has spent years in exploring the ancient dwellings of the people who preceded us centuries ago in many states of the southern and western region of our country. I'm sure many of you have read his books, and that you have been looking forward to the opportunity of seeing and hearing him in person. It is my pleasure to introduce to you Dr. Jones, noted author, scientist, and lecturer, who will speak to you now."

Not a bad introduction so far as the content is concerned, is it? But the sequence and the build-up are terrible. Now, suppose it had been said in this way:

"Ladies and Gentlemen: All about us here in the great southwest are the remains of the homes and the buildings left by the Cliff Dwellers who lived here thousands of years ago. Doubtless many of you have explored them or read about them and wondered what kind of people they were, how they lived, what they did, how far their civilization progressed, and what happened to them. Today we have with us a man who can give us the answers to these and many other questions about this ancient civilization which apparently disappeared so dramatically and mysteriously; a man who has spent a lifetime studying these ancient people and telling their story in books and on the lecture platform. He brings us this fascinating story today, 'The Cliff Dwellers of the Southwest.' That noted scientist, author, and lecturer, the curator of the National Museum, Dr. Melville Jones."

Don't you like that one better? Notice the sequence and how the story progresses. First *about* the subject, next *about* the man, then *why* he speaks with authority, then specifically *what* his position is, and finally his *name*.

Have you ever listened to the announcer at a prize fight introducing the principals and the visiting notables? His sequence is perfect. Tone down his inflection and the exaggerated emphasis on the name, and you've got the pattern down pat.

Now, after you've spoken your piece, continue your selling by what you do and how you do it. Start the applause. Remain standing and keep the applause going until the speaker takes his place on the platform. Give and maintain the impression that you're presenting them something worth-while. If you sit down and let the applause die, you say by your actions, "Well, here he is, I hope you like him, but I have my doubts." Let there be no doubt either in your manner or your actions.

Now that you've been told what to do, here are some things to avoid. These are the things you should never do:

1. *Never make a speech yourself.* You're the master of ceremonies; not the speaker. The prima donna follows you. Five minutes at the outside should be your time limit, and the more you can cut that short, the better.

2. *Avoid being too ponderous* and too dignified. Be natural, direct, brief; keep your introduction moving.

3. *Don't overdo your enthusiasm.* Be sincere, and limit yourself to what you can say sincerely.

4. *Avoid cliches,* especially, "The speaker we have with us today needs no introduction to this group." If he doesn't, what are you doing up there?

5. *Don't talk about yourself.* You're not selling you, you're selling a speaker.

6. *Don't tell jokes* unless you can really put them over and you're quite sure the speaker can top them and use them in starting his talk.

7. *Don't let the name of the speaker slip out until you're ready for it.* Remember, that's the *last* thing you say.

8. *Finally, never, never apologize for the speaker* who was sent to substitute for the one you hoped to have. It doesn't make any difference if Mr. Big has sent his seventh assistant to read Mr. Big's message; don't apologize. The most horrible introductions of all are those that begin, "I'm sure you are all as sorry as I am that the Governor was unable to be here and instead we have his secretary, etc., etc."

Just keep in mind what your main objectives are in making introductions and these do's and don'ts will all fall into their proper places. Remember,

1. You're selling the speaker and his speech to the audience.

2. You're getting them interested and attentive by creating suspense and building up to a climax.

3. You are creating an atmosphere that will put both speaker and audience in the proper mood.

4. You are doing this by being brief, sincere, and natural.

Using Speakers

While properly briefing the speaker beforehand and giving him the right kind of an introduction to launch him into his talk are important factors in making the most effective use of speakers, there still remain some things to be done.

The most common error in arranging a program of any kind is to cram it too full. The most devastating situation that any speaker and any chairman has to face is an audience which has sat through two hours of introductions, presentations of awards, speeches by practically everyone else, and then with the time all but gone, have to put on the main show of the evening. Programs are always too long. If you are doing the planning, decide on what you think would be about right and then red pencil half of it. In any event, don't wear out your audience with a bunch of side-show attractions before producing your main event.

If you really want your audience to ask questions after the speaker has finished, plan for it. Instruct the speaker to plan his talk so as to leave some questions unanswered, to keep his talk short. And make it a practice to have a planned question period. The give and take between audience and speaker is generally far more interesting to both than a set speech that says everything. Don't forget, also, to use the buzz session where appropriate to make sure that questions are forthcoming.

All too often a speaker is left with a rather let-down feeling after he has finished his speech and the applause dies away. It is only ordinary politeness, of course, for you as chairman to *thank* him in behalf of the audience for taking the time to prepare and present his speech. However, if you really want to do the job up right, take time when you get home or get back to the office to write him a personal note expressing your appreciation again and saying a few kind words about his talk.

NO. 7

HOW TO MAKE CLEAR EXPLANATIONS

Even though this book is dedicated to group processes and to the proposition that true leadership consists of helping people to think through their own problems, there are times when the leader must assist in clarifying the thinking of the group and its members. Thus the ability to explain is an important one to the group leader. Unfortunately little attention has been given to this process and many attempts to explain lead only to further confusion. The person who defined "letting the cat out of the bag" as "the unpremeditated, extemporaneous promulgation of information towards which one should have been more reticently inclined" did very little to clarify this process.

Lest you think that explaining is a simple process, try answering such questions as "What is Rotary?", "What are the Soroptomists? What do they do?", "What is this Parent-Teacher organization?", "What is the FFA; how does it differ from 4-H Club work?"

If this doesn't stump you, have you tried recently explaining to your junior high stripling how to extract the square root of a number or tried to help your teen age daughter with her algebra?

When you explain—When you give an explanation, the end product is *understanding* on the part of the person or persons to whom it is directed. Understanding is a knowledge of *why*, not just *how*, but how *and* why. A person understands only when he thinks through the process himself. Basically you cannot explain anything to anyone unless he thinks along with you. You can understand when you can visualize relationships and make associations.

Furthermore, understanding is largely a matter of cause —effect relationships. You understand when given a cause

68

you can predict the effect. You understand when seeing an effect you can reason back to the cause. Now as to the method of explaining, the steps in making a clear explanation are these:

1. Describe clearly or show the end product or the ultimate goal.

If you are explaining a process, start with exhibiting the end result of that process. If you are explaining a program, describe the main objective or objectives of the program.

2. State and explain the *principles* on which the program or process is based.

3. Give a broad overview of it before you begin any detailed explanation of the steps or parts.

4. Follow with a detailed explanation of each step (if a process) or each part of the whole.

   (a) At each step or in each part show and bring out clearly applications and relationships to things with which your audience already is familiar.
   (b) Relate each step to the basic principles which were stated in Step 2.
   (c) Wherever possible make your explanation visual rather than verbal. Use pictures, graphs, charts, or mock-ups to illustrate.

5. Summarize, reviewing the steps or parts briefly and showing how they relate to the end product and the principles involved.

You will note in this procedure outlined above that you start your explanation by showing or describing an *effect* and that the subsequent steps outline first broadly and then in detail the causes leading up to the effect.

To illustrate, here is an explanation of the process of osmosis:

1. Describe or show end product.

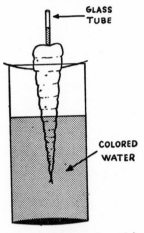

GLASS TUBE

COLORED WATER

Plants must get water from the soil in order to live and grow. They get this water by means of a process called "osmosis." In the drawing you see a carrot with a tube inserted into its top and sealed in place. The carrot is partly immersed in a container of colored water. In some way this colored water has entered the carrot and exerted enough pressure to force its way up into the tube. This is the result of "osmosis."

2. State and explain the principle or principles on which the process or program is based.

All materials tend to move from an area of high concentration to an area of low concentration. This is the principle of *diffusion*. If you put a few drops of perfume on a handkerchief, the odor soon pervades the whole room. You're all familiar with this. If you put a drop or two of ink into a glass of water, the ink will gradually diffuse through the whole contents of the glass.

Osmosis is a type of diffusion limited to water. We generally think of water solely as a material used to *dilute* other fluids. However, in order to understand osmosis, you must think of pure water as being *highly concentrated water,* and water with sugar or salt dissolved in it as less concentrated *water*—less pure.

If you do not get this concept, you can easily convince yourself that *osmosis* is the *reverse* of diffusion instead of a *kind* of diffusion.

3. Give a broad overview or description of the process.

In general, osmosis is the process which occurs when we have a semi-permeable membrane on one side of which we have pure water (highly concentrated water) and on the other side water diluted with or containing salts, sugars, etc. Under these conditions, the *purer* water passes through this membrane to increase the percentage of water in the fluid on the other side of the membrane.

A "semi-permeable" membrane is one that permits water to pass through it but prevents fluid containing less water from moving in the opposite direction. It allows the molecules of water to pass through it, but stops molecules of other substances.

4. Present a detailed explanation of the process, relating each phase or step to the basic principles involved.

Plants require water in order to live and grow. Most water enters plants through the root tips and root hairs. This water is in the soil and contains some plant food and minerals in solution. The outer tissues of the roots of these plants act like semipermeable membranes. Therefore, water from the soil moves into the roots and becomes available to the plant, because the water in the soil contains *less* foreign material and is more highly concentrated *water* than the fluid in the roots themselves. Referring back to the principle involved, this happens because all materials move from an area of high concentration to an area of low concentration.

You have all seen spots in a field of grass or grain as you drove along the highway where the ground is bare and no plants have grown. If this ground appears to be covered with a deposit of white material or is lighter in color than the surrounding soil, it is probable that the soil in these areas is highly alkaline, and these bare areas are often called "alkali spots."

Now, can you explain these bare spots? Why do plants fail to grow in this kind of soil? Could it be that the plants die because of lack of water? Could it be that they simply can't get water from the alkaline soil regardless of how much water is available?

Consider these facts: Alkali salts dissolve easily in water. Water falling on alkali soils or put onto this soil in the form of irrigation water, dissolves the alkali salts present in the soil, and soon becomes impure.

No longer is this water more highly concentrated than that within the plant. Therefore, it will not pass into the roots or will enter only in insufficient amounts to keep plants alive. The process of osmosis is no longer taking place.

5. Summarize.

Thus, plants grow and thrive only because they obtain the water and the dissolved plant food which they need through this one-way passage into the roots.

They obtain these vital materials because by diffusion all materials tend to move from an area of high concentration to an area of low concentration. Just as water will dilute lemonade, water itself can be diluted by adding foreign materials to it. Water moves into plants and supports life and growth because of osmosis, a type of diffusion limited to water.

So when you attempt to explain, don't make the mistake of launching immediately into a step by step description. Instead:

1. Show or describe the end product.

2. State and explain the basic principles.

3. Give a broad overview.

Then and only then should you go into details. Until your listener or listeners can visualize the end result and the process or program as a whole, the details are meaningless and serve to confuse rather than to clarify.

Remember, too that "one picture is worth a thousand words" and visualize your explanations wherever possible. Keep in mind that understanding comes through establishing relationships between principles and applications and between effects and causes.

HOW TO PRESENT PROPOSALS
INVOLVING CHANGE

In one of the previous chapters delineating leadership roles, it was stated that a leader is generally an initiator—that a leader is constantly looking ahead, sensing the need for change, and bringing proposals to his colleagues or his clientele involving change. Many persons, by virtue of their professional positions are continually faced with the problem of how to present proposals for changes of policy, of procedure, and of practice. Their problem is not just one of how to present these proposals, but how to present them in such a way that people will accept, approve, and take action accordingly. Similarly the leader in civic and public affairs is faced with the same task.

Nor is this responsibility limited to those in the top echelons of administrative authority or to the elected leaders of any group, for the role of initiator is not limited to leadership alone, but should and must be played by many if there is to be real progress. Thus, the teacher who needs a piece of new equipment for his laboratory; the department head who wants an increased budget for his department; any member of the organization or group who feels that a change is needed in policy or method is faced with the same problem—that of presenting his proposal or request in such a way that it may be adopted.

This is the last and perhaps the most difficult and complex of the leadership skills to be discussed in this book. In contrast to skill in making explanations, where the end product was that of developing understanding, here one must secure understanding plus affirmative action, and action which involves change.

Most of us seem instinctively to resist change. Most of

us find it easier and more comfortable to follow the same familiar routine way of doing things than to venture into new untried paths. Sometimes, even when we become convinced of the value or even the necessity of change, we resist it. The story is told of the farmer who was approached by a county agricultural agent and asked to try a new and improved way of feeding his livestock. After all the convincing arguments as to how this practice would enable him to cut his costs, obtain greater gains, make it possible for him to market his stock sooner, the farmer is supposed to have replied, "Heck, I'm not half as good a farmer now as I know how to be!"

Just why do people resist change? What are the things which block it? What are the attitudes, the feelings that obstruct and prevent acceptance of change? Following are some of the reasons why it is often so difficult to gain acceptance of a new idea, a new policy, a new program.

—Fear. Fear of the unknown; fear of the consequences; fear that the change may affect us adversely.

—Distrust. Distrust of the motives back of the proposed change; distrust and fear of the motives of the one proposing the change.

—Lack of understanding. We dislike ambiguous situations. We like to know where we stand. We are comfortable in the old familiar way of doing things; it is difficult for us to see our place in the new order. When we have not had the opportunity to participate in planing the change, we do not have as complete an understanding of it as do the proponent or proponents of the new proposal.

—Dislike of being considered "different." We resist change when it requires us to be different—different from our colleagues, from our associates. We resist change when it involves a procedure radically different from that followed by other similar organizations and groups.

These are some of the major factors which block change. Perhaps these may be summed up in the statement that all of us have the urge to protect and preserve that which we now have.

Some of the other factors which should be considered when we attempt to implement change are:

—That older people are less receptive to change, generally, than are younger persons.

—That educated persons tend to be more receptive than those with less education; that the educated person may be swayed more by reason—by facts, while those with less education may be governed more by their emotions.

—That persons who have taken a public stand on an issue are more difficult to change than those who have not.

—That we may accept milder changes more readily than radical ones; and gradual changes more readily than abrupt.

—That we tend to identify the change with the person who is proposing it. If we believe in him and trust him personally, we tend to accept what he proposes; if we fear and distrust him, we transfer this same attitude to the change with which he is identified.

Thus, it is easy to see why gaining acceptance of change is so difficult, and why proposals for change must be so carefully thought through and presented.

Following is an outline which may be of value in planning and presenting requests for change when it falls to your lot to do so:

Presentation	*Purpose*
I. INTRODUCTION	
1. Express appreciation for privilege of presenting proposal.	1. To develop interest and gain attention.
2. Give short historical background to and show need for proposal.	2. To gain a favorable first impression of you, your motives, and your objectives.
3. State and stress objective of change, and secure approval of it.	3. To lay a foundation for your proposal.

Presentation	*Purpose*
II. STATEMENT OF PROPOSAL	
1. Relate proposal to objective.	1. To develop understanding; to make it entirely clear just what you are requesting.
2. Present all pertinent facts and data.	
3. Use appropriate visual aids.	
III. DISCUSSION	
1. Present arguments both for and against proposal.	1. To show that the proposal has been considered thoroughly.
2. Refute arguments opposing it and show that they are unimportant.	2. To show that evidence supporting it far outweighs arguments against it.
3. Present alternative proposal if opposition obviously too strong.	3. To anticipate and answer questions concerning it.
IV. CONCLUSION	
1. Summarize and emphasize main points supporting proposal.	1. To leave hearers with a summation of the important supporting evidence in favor of the proposal.
2. Request consideration and favorable action.	2. To gain sympathy for the request and ultimate favorable action.

It should be emphasized that even though you planned your presentation according to this outline and attempted to follow it, you would seldom be allowed to do so completely. There are certain to be questions raised and comments made which would cause you to deviate from your set plan. It may well be said that such a plan is only a point of departure and is made "to deviate from." However, to make such a plan will cause you to think through your proposal and enable you to support it more intelligently under fire.

Regardless of whether or not you follow the suggested plan, there are certain key points which should be observed in your presentation.

1. Your motives and the objectives of your proposal must be unassailable and unquestionable. It must be made clear to your hearers from the outset that this is true, and

they must accept this. Otherwise your plan is doomed for failure.

2. Present the facts and arguments both for and against your request, especially if you anticipate resistance and objections. Doing so will serve to allay any fears that you may not have considered all aspects and consequences of your project. If, however, you feel that your audience is friendly and already favorably disposed toward it, present only the arguments for your proposal.

3. Present the strongest arguments supporting your proposal last. Start with the weaker and less important evidence favorable to your plan; follow with any arguments against it; finish with a refutation of opposing evidence and with your strongest arguments supporting it. Last impressions are likely to be lasting.

4. Assemble and have with you all of the facts and data concerning your proposal. If your hearers are mature and well educated rely primarily upon facts to convince them.

5. Make your proposal explicit and specific. Remember that we dislike ambiguous situations, and generally want to know exactly what is involved before accepting.

6. Prepare, assemble, and use appropriate visual aids— charts, pictures, maps, catalogs, diagrams. All contribute to understanding.

7. Gear your presentation to your audience and their known characteristics, attitudes, and opinions. Age, maturity, level of education, whether or not they may have taken a public stand on your proposal—all should be considered.

8. Check and recheck what are known to be the major reasons why people resist change. Make certain that your presentation is calculated to remove these blocks insofar as possible.

9. Close with an appeal for a sympathetic consideration of your request, and for appropriate action.

10. If at any stage in the discussion, it becomes apparent to you that your hearers have serious unshakable objections

to your proposal, and that it probably will not receive favorable action, be prepared to submit alternative courses of action.

If, for example, they obviously feel that the change involved is too great to be effected at once, ask for approval of parts of it—the preliminary steps, perhaps. If they appear to fear the consequences of such a change, suggest that it be tried experimentally in a limited way before final and complete adoption.

If they agree that a change seems to be in order and that the objectives and general idea of your proposal are acceptable, but object to certain details ask for approval of your proposal in principle, and for their suggestions regarding the details.

Do not be discouraged if you fail. The mere fact that they have listened to you; that you have had an opportunity to present your thoughts may bring favorable action later, when they have had time of think over your proposal. Above all, do not try to force acceptance. In the words of Stuart Chase, "Use a fly rod, not a club to overcome resistance."

CHAPTER IV

KINDS OF MEETINGS AND WHERE TO USE THEM

It is extremely and obviously important to use the type of meeting best adapted to the situation. The number of persons involved, the nature of the subject or problem under discussion, even the meeting place may well determine the kind of a meeting which would fit best. More important is the purpose of the meeting. You would not use a sixteen inch cannon to kill a sparrow nor an air rifle to bring down an elephant, but many of us do just as ridiculous things in choosing procedures for the meetings we conduct.

Most of the group meetings with which we will be concerned fall naturally into two classes:

1. *Those in which a group of people under the guidance of a leader, discuss, think through, and attempt to work out the solution of a problem or problems in which they are mutually interested.* In this group are found the following kinds of meetings:

The Round Table. Other names given this type of meeting are "small group discussions," "informal discussion," or just "group discussion." The round table is a discussion in a group small enough so that all may participate. All present are on a basis of equality from start to finish. There is a leader who is a member of the group. To him the group has delegated the responsibility of making it go, of setting the stage, of raising the opening questions, keeping the discussion on the track, and of summarizing from time to time the progress of the group in thinking through the question.

Dr. Benjamin E. Mallary, formerly Lecturer in Education at the University of California, lists eight characteristics of the round table or small conference group:

Members and leaders of round table discussion groups should be relaxed and informal.

1. They are composed of people who have mutual problems.
2. The members desire to solve their problems together.
3. They agree to exchange and pool experiences.
4. The subject under discussion is within their experience.
5. Problems are to be solved by thinking them through together.
6. They meet to learn together—not to be instructed.
7. They group themselves informally, facing each other.
8. The group is small, generally from 12 to 25 persons.

On page 80 is a picture of such a group in action. Obviously it was not posed for the benefit of the photographer. All are relaxed, informal, and apparently enjoying themselves.

The round table is the ideal discussion group. It is the perfect medium for democratic thinking and action. It should be used for considering and solving common, every-day problems of organizations, civic, business, and professional groups. Use the round table in informal surroundings, with small groups up to thirty in size, where they may sit facing each other. Do not use it as a medium for the leader to inform and do not try to make it function in a formal seating arrangement with the group seated in rows facing the leader.

The Business Conference. Like the round table, the business conference should be used to bring the thinking of a group of workers to bear on a problem of concern to them. If the purpose of the meeting is to afford an opportunity for someone in authority to inform or instruct the group as to company policy, it is not a conference, and should not be so designated. It should be used when there is a sincere desire on the part of the "boss" to share with his subordinates the setting up of policies or the solution of problems. If, in a business conference, there is a feeling or a realization among the members that there is only one vote that really counts in arriving at decisions, better not hold them at all. If you, as the leader, are going to make the decisions anyway, why waste their time and yours?

The business conference has many of the same characteristics of the round table. The setting, however, is generally the conference room of the business or professional establishment, and the leader not a member of the group, but generally their immediate supervisor. Instead of facing each other in the informality of a circle of chairs, they characteristically are seated around the conference table, complete with the usual pencils, scratch pads, and ash trays.

Typical of the business conference is the group pictured on page 83. From the mien of the conferees, this seems to be "strictly business" in contrast to the round table group.

The Formal Business Meeting. This is familiar to all of you. It is conducted according to the formal rules of parliamentary procedure, more or less, depending upon how familiar the chairman is with these rules. The chairman raps for attention, calls the meeting to order. The secretary reads the minutes of the previous meeting. The minutes are approved as read. Next comes the reports of standing committees, the consideration of old business, then of the new, with formal motions and seconds, discussions pro and con of the actions proposed, and voice votes on formal proposals. The routine is all too well known to merit further description here. However, this is one of the types of group meetings in which the members through democratic processes discuss courses of action and make decisions, and many of the same rules of effective group leadership and dynamics do apply.

The purpose of the formal business meeting is obvious. Its function is to make and put on record formal action on procedures and policies. There is little limitation as to the size of the group. Five hundred may participate as well as fifty.

The Workshop. During the past few years, especially in the ranks of the professional educators, the terms "workshop" or "workshop conference" have come into use to describe a type of group meeting where relatively large groups

A business conference or staff meeting brings the thinking of the group to bear on a problem of concern to them.

meet to discuss a common problem or problems. Essentially it differs from the round table or informal type of group meeting only in size, scope, and organization. The fundamental processes and procedures are the same. In fact, the first six of the characteristics of the round table or small conference group listed on page 81 apply equally well to the workshop or workshop conference.

The workshop may have from fifty to several hundred people in attendance. Its deliberations may last a week instead of an hour and a half.

Regardless of the fact that the group is larger, the problem probably greater in scope, and the time involved longer, the workshop, too:

1. Is composed of people who have mutual problems.
2. The members desire to solve their problems together.
3. They agree to exchange and pool experience.
4. The subject under discussion is within their experience.
5. They meet to learn together; not to be instructed.
6. Their problems are to be solved by thinking them through together.

Since the numbers making up the group are so large, they must be broken up into smaller groups in order to think through and discuss their problems effectively.

2. *Those meetings where people meet or are brought together to be informed about a subject by a person or group of persons who (presumably) know more about it than they do.*

In this class of group meetings, while the members of the group meet primarily to become informed on a certain subject, all of them utilize group or audience participation. In general they include more people, last longer, are more formal in organization, and involve somewhat less participation. It should be said, however, that their effectiveness will vary in direct relation to which real audience participation is obtained, and how well such participation is handled.

The Panel. The panel is a modified round table discussion carried on before and for the benefit of a larger group making up the audience. The panel itself is composed of a leader and from two or three to twelve members. The panel members generally sit in a semicircle or in a row on a platform facing the audience and discuss a problem in the same manner that a similar sized group would in a round-table discussion. The leader also performs the same functions and plays the same role that he would in a small group discussion, except that toward the end of the allotted time he may invite the audience to join in. The panel discussion is conversational at all times.

The panel (sometimes called a "jury panel") is often confused with a symposium, which is described below. A series of brief talks on a given subject cannot truly be called a panel.

The Symposium. In a symposium, the same general physical arrangement is used as in the panel, where several people and a leader or "moderator" are seated on the platform facing the audience. However, the similarity goes no further. Instead of a round-table discussion, there is a series of brief set speeches with the leader introducing each speaker in turn. After all of the speakers have delivered their talks, the leader conducts an open discussion of the general subject or problem with the audience participating. Generally audience participation is limited to questions addressed to the symposium speakers.

On page 140 will be found a picture of a typical symposium arrangement with the leader and the speakers identified by name plates for the benefit of the audience.

The Forum. The forum usually involves a lecture followed by a certain amount of audience participation, generally in the form of questions. The leader introduces the lecturer and after his talk is finished, invites questions either written or expressed orally from the floor, which he directs to the speaker for answers or discussion. When the audience is small enough and there is sufficient time, expressions of opinion from members of the audience on the subject under discussion may also be invited. Ordinarily, however, this type of group meeting provides for a degree of audience participation little greater than the ordinary lecture.

The Conference. Many professional and business meetings are held under this title. The professional conference bears much the same relation to the panel, the forum, and the symposium that the workshop does to the group discussion. It usually involves a large group, lasts for several days, and may involve many if not all of the types of group meetings from lectures and forums to small group discussions. Generally those in attendance have similar interests, experience, and vocations, and meet for the dual purpose of receiving instruction or information, and of thinking through common problems.

In summary:

1. For small groups (15-25 persons) the informal round table discussion procedure is recommended, whether the subject be business or the common everyday problems of living.

2. For larger groups, the workshop and the work conference have many of the same values of democratic participation as the round table and provides the same opportunities for group thinking.

3. For making formal, recorded decisions, the business meeting affords the best medium.

4. For informing larger groups, use the panel, the symposium, or the forum to get the benefits of audience participation plus the views of experts.

CHAPTER V

LEADING ROUND TABLE DISCUSSIONS

Much has been written about discussion groups and how to lead them. However, the small group meeting is so important a factor in life today that the techniques and procedures for conducting this type of meeting effectively bear re-statement here.

It has been said that modern life is group life; that the individual who attempts to play the lone wolf and to get results solely through his individual efforts is not only becoming a rarity, but he is handicapping himself unnecessarily. Membership in a functioning group is a far better medium for his efforts.

Two heads are better than one, and ten heads are better than two, especially in finding the solutions and the answers to social problems. Quite often a really skilled person may solve a technical difficulty in business, engineering, or agriculture more effectively unaided than through group action. Indeed most of these problems are solved in this way, but not all. Research has shown, however, that even in non-social problems, group thinking may be more effective than individual effort. Besides, this is a democracy, and group thinking is the foundation of democracy and an important, not to say, essential factor in its functioning. In the words of Harrison Elliott:

"If persons would do what they are told, and if leaders could agree as to what they should be told, we might dispense with this democratic process of deliberation and simply employ a few experts to tell the rest of us what to do on personal, racial, international, and other questions. When once started on a venture in democracy, however, people demand a right to form their own judgments on the basis of evidence. The only way to insure the future of democracy is to secure such ex-

87

perience in this process that people will become able to make increasingly better decisions."[1]

To bring it closer to home, the everyday problems of communities, municipalities, and lesser organizations within communities are being more and more frequently settled and action started by discussing these problems in small groups. Should there be a zoning problem confronting the City Planning Commission, the people directly involved in that section of town are called together to talk it over. The need for a summer recreation program is vaguely sensed by people in general, but the planning is turned over to a small group of representatives from interested organizations.

Conferences, conventions, workshops, most meetings involving large numbers of people, eventually break down into small discussion groups where the real thinking is done and where decisions are made. In national and in state government; in large organizations of any kind, the bulk of the work is done by committees. So much is this true that a good deal of fun is poked at this practice. Witness this definition. "A committee is composed of a group of people who, individually, can do nothing, but who meet and decide that nothing can be done." Fortunately that's not quite true, else the practice would have been discontinued long since. But committees are essentially small discussion groups, small enough so that the processes of informal group thinking, of talking things over, enable this smaller group to accomplish what the larger one could and can not.

So it takes small group meetings, many of them; formal committees assigned specific problems, and informal groups just getting together to talk things over, to make things go, to keep them going, and to make possible our modern and democratic way of life.

Now, what does it take to make them function effectively? What are the ear-marks of a good group discussion? Who does what to make it function?

Let's take the second of these questions first.

---

[1] Harrison S. Elliott, "The Why and How of Group Discussion."

What are the ear-marks of a good discussion and a good group? They are these:

1. A good group discussion is *informal.* Everyone is at ease, spirits are high, there is friendly disagreement, everyone has a good time.

2. *Everyone participates* and plays his own particular leadership role. The discussion is scattered among all members. No one dominates. All profit from experiences of others.

3. *It accomplishes something.* It arrives at decisions and decides what to do or what not to do. It doesn't just go round in circles getting nowhere.

4. *It creates a "we" spirit and attitude.* It welds a number of individuals into a group with a common purpose. It fosters a feeling of belonging, and of co-operation.

5. *It stimulates thinking.* It encourages each member to do his own thinking on problems common to members of the group.

6. *The members are interested.* They are interested in the problem under discussion, in the meeting itself, in the interchange of ideas. They are interested to the extent that they cooperate to make it a success.

7. *It checks up on itself.* It examines objectively how well the group and the individual members are working, cooperating, and progressing.

This is what happens when we have good group dynamics; when we have an effective meeting. This is the end product we're after. Now how does this sort of thing happen? Who does what to make it happen? It takes the leadership roles well played, which were outlined in Chapter III. In its simplest form, it takes just a leader and a group with the other leadership roles emerging unplanned in the persons of members of the group. From this it can grow into a full-fledged leadership team with a leader, a recorder, an observer, a consultant, and the group. Many are conducted with just a leader or a leader and a recorder. As the group matures, as problems multiply, and as occasion demands, the others may be added; the observer to check upon and evaluate progress; the consultant to give facts which may not be available to other members of the group.

If the leader chooses to operate alone, he must be prepared to play these other roles as the need arises, so let us list the duties of each of these members of the leadership team so that they can be checked off, whether done by one person or four.

Who Does What in a Group Discussion?

The Leader:
—Helps the group get acquainted.
—Establishes and maintains an informal atmosphere.
—States the problem or helps group state it.
—Stimulates and directs the discussion toward the solution of the problem; keeps it moving.
—Promotes participation by all members.
—Notes contributions of members on blackboard or chart.
—Encourages the timid soul; discourages the monopolizer and his ilk.
—Stimulates thinking; sees that all sides of the question are heard.
—Helps the group check up on itself by using and assisting the recorder and observer.
—Keeps in the background; avoids imposing his own views on the group.
—Summarizes when necessary.
—Brings the group to a conclusion and to a plan of action.

The Recorder:
—Keeps a record of the main problems, facts, and decisions brought out in the discussion.
—Summarizes and reports at the end of the session or beginning of next.
—Summarizes discussion from time to time when requested.
—Prepares a final group report.

The Observer:
—Pays special attention to how the group and its leaders operate and progress.

—Checks on the amount and kind of participation by members.

—Checks on the effectiveness of the leader.

—Checks on the thinking and the attitude of the group.

—Reports to the group what he has observed from time to time, during the meeting, and at the close.

The Consultant:

—Supplies information and facts at the request of the group or leader.

—Cites experiences at request or when it is appropriate to the discussion.

—Assists leader in seeing that all pertinent facts are considered.

—Assists leader in keeping group moving toward decisions and solutions.

The Group Member:

—Contributes ideas and suggestions pertaining to the problem.

—Assumes various leadership roles as the need arises.

—Gives the group the benefit of his experience.

—Listens to what others say and respects their contributions.

—Keeps "on the subject" with his comments.

—Avoids monopolizing the discussion or the other extreme of saying nothing.

—Cooperates with the group to solve a common problem.

—Keeps his own prejudices and his own personal aims from influencing him unduly.

—Works with other members to help the group progress and to become a unit.

Important as your role is in leading an informal group discussion, the less you have to do after the discussion starts, the more effective a job you will be doing. The chances are that the group you will be leading will be made up of a dozen of your neighbors, associates, and friends, people who know something about the subject under discussion; who have common problems and want to thresh them out together. They have met to learn together, to exchange and pool experiences; not to be instructed by you.

Let's discuss what you should do before the discussion begins, as it starts, as it progresses, and as it closes.

Before the discussion begins.

1. Be there ahead of time; before the others get there, if possible.

2. Arrange the room so that the setting is right. Be your own expeditor. See that the room is neither too hot nor too cold; that there is good light; that there is a blackboard or wall chart paper available; that *your* chair is located where it ought to be; and the rest of the chairs arranged satisfactorily.

3. Take a few moments to review mentally what you are going to do, how you are going to start the discussion. Jot down a few notes if you wish, such as:

    a. Your opening remarks.

    b. A clear-cut brief statement of the problem.

    c. Some pertinent facts regarding the problem (to be used only if necessary to supplement those supplied by the group).

    d. Some possible conclusions or solutions.

4. Remind yourself again of the four commandments for leading a discussion group:

BECOME AND REMAIN ONE OF THE GROUP.

GET THEM TALKING AND WORKING TOGETHER.

GIVE THEM SOMETHING TO THINK ABOUT.

HELP THEM HELP THEMSELVES.

5. As the others arrive, greet them and treat them as though they were visitors to your home. Chat with them, relax, be one of them, introduce those who may be strangers.

As the meeting starts.

1. Make a brief introductory statement as to the purpose of the meeting—a *brief* one.

2. Get acquainted with them and get them acquainted with each other if necessary. Use the methods discussed in Chapter IV.

3. State the problem that they have met to discuss and solve. State it in the form of a question. Define and clarify it yourself, or

4. Have them do it. Ask, "Just exactly what do we want to accomplish? What do we want to have happen? What's the best possible outcome?"

5. Ask for tentative or possible solutions. Get as many as possible.

As it progresses.

1. Call for facts and arguments for and against each possible solution.

2. Keep the discussion centered on the problem and on the track.

3. Stimulate and encourage participation by everyone.

4. Summarize when necessary, contribute facts when called for, but resist that impulse to do their thinking and talking for them.

5. Make sure every possible solution has a hearing and is fairly weighed, evaluated, and discussed.

6. When agreement has been reached on the best answer or answers, make a brief final summary and bring the meeting to a close or proceed to a new problem.

The procedure outlined is typical of the discussion centering around a problem stated by you as a leader. However, quite often, maybe more frequently, you as a leader may suggest only a subject or topic and draw out the problem from the group.

When this happens your procedure in opening the meeting is different in that you lead the group to decide upon and state the problem as well as to define and clarify it.

Special Devices for the Leader

The following techniques should be a part of every discussion leader's bag of tricks. Their effective use may well make the difference between a really worthwhile discussion and one that reaches the rock bottom of utter boredom for everyone and stays there.

Questioning. Two general types of questions should be included in your kit of tools, the so-called "overhead" or general type of question and the "direct" question. The *overhead* question often calls for a "yes" or "no" answer. It is directed to the group as a whole and is often used to point out or suggest a line of thought or a possible answer.

Some examples are:

"Can we *expect* people generally to be enthusiastic about any program which will increase their taxes?

"*Should* we always try to get absolute perfection?"

The overhead question is also used at the beginning of a discussion. In this case, it may be a statement of the main problem and is directed to the group as a whole. In this case it probably will not be a question answerable by "yes" or "no," and does not suggest a line of thought.

The *direct* question is usually directed to an individual in the group. This type of question may be used to draw out the timid person who isn't contributing, to secure information about the point under discussion or to bring a scattered, wandering discussion back to the point.

In using this kind of a question, keep in mind these things:

1. State the question first, pause, then name the person whom you wish to answer it. Never the name first and then the question, for two obvious reasons. You'll scare the timid soul, and no one but the person named will listen to the question.

2. Use questions beginning with "why," "how," and "which" rather than with "what." "What" calls for a factual answer only, not for thought. Ask "what" only when you're digging for facts.

3. Generally avoid leading questions that suggest their own answers.

4. Give them time to think when you ask a question. Don't be in a hurry to get an answer, and don't be afraid of the silence that accompanies such a pause. If they're silent, they're thinking, and that's what you want. So, after every question—pause—don't hurry them—then recognize by a

nod to the person who seems to have an answer, or the one you want to answer it.

Turning questions back to the group. If you answer a question asked by a member of the group you automatically stop discussion; inhibit it rather than encourage it. Therefore, when you are asked a question, refer it to the group as a whole or to some member of the group rather than answering it yourself. Your job is to stimulate discussion. So, when a member asks a question and directs it seemingly to you as leader, simply turn it back to the group as an overhead question to all or to some one person who indicates that he or she may have something to say about it. Only if no one has any ideas or any answers should you undertake an answer.

Keeping arguments balanced. This is really not a good title for this specific skill or technique, because it involves far more than the words imply. Actually this is the most important skill for you who would become really skillful in leading a group discussion. When you can do this, when you have mastered this technique, you will have crossed the line which separates the really good from the ordinary.

There are at least two sides to every question; sometimes more, and it is your duty as a discussion leader to see that each side has a fair hearing. Furthermore, a discussion never gets really interesting until some controversy arises. This is how to aid and abet such a controversy in happening and then keep it under control. We'll use a specific example.

Suppose you're having a meeting of the fathers of boys in a Boy Scout troop. You raise the question, "Do you think we ought to plan a dads' work day to clean up the grounds around the Scout Cabin and do some needed repair work on the cabin itself?" Now, if you let nature take its course after asking a question like that, here's what probably will happen.

Some dad will come up with a statement somewhat like this: "I think we should. The cabin is in pretty bad shape. The roof leaks, there's hardly a window in the place that hasn't at least one pane of glass broken, there's no place to store projects that the boys are working on, and the wiring needs overhauling. The yard is a mess. The weeds are over a foot high, the shrubs need pruning, there ought to be a new flag pole put up. Why, there's all kinds of jobs that need doing and that we dads can do. I don't think there's any question about it. We ought to organize a work day, get every dad out, and give both the cabin and the grounds a thorough going over. I say we ought to get at it."

Now, as a leader, where do you go from there? You've got your answer, and you've got a lot of reasons for at least that side of the question. Now, how are you going to bring out the other side in the face of such an impressive array of sustaining evidence? It would take a pretty hardy soul, wouldn't it, to take issue with the answer that was given? As a result, either your discussion would die right there, or else, after a lot of pumping from you, you might get some-one to present the other side of the question and some reasons why a work day might not be the thing.

Yes, something went wrong. This is what happened and what you should prevent happening. You asked a question and then allowed one person to give one side of the question and his *reasons* in detail for his answer *before* you found out what the opinions were that were held by *every* member of the group. As a result, the negative answer never had a hearing, and it is reasonable to assume that not everyone was immediately enthusiastic about the prospect of a dad's work day.

Suppose, instead, you had handled it another way. After you raised the overhead question, "Do you think we should plan a dads' work day, etc.?", you added another question, "What do each of you think about that? Don't give any reasons, yet, but just your immediate opinion."

You very quickly get an answer from everyone, perhaps even asking for a show of hands. You find that of the fifteen dads nine to seem to favor a work day and six of them don't. You select one of the minority group and ask him to give his reasons. He finishes, and immediately one of the proponents of the work day speaks up and states the case for cleaning up the cabin and the yard. (He'll do it, because he feels the majority is back of him.) Now, another of the minority comes to the aid of the first speaker—and—you've got a good discussion going. Furthermore, you're seeing to it that *both* sides of the question have a hearing.

Here, in brief, is the procedure you should follow to get a spirited discussion of an overhead question or a problem, and to make sure that all phases of the problem and all sides of the question have a hearing and are considered:

1. State the problem or overhead question. Give them a moment to think it over.
2. Call for answers or opinions without reasons.
3. Get everyone on record as to his tentative or immediate opinion regarding the question.
4. Call for one or more of the minority to give reasons for their opinions. If they fail to make a good case, help them by means of questions which point toward arguments they may have overlooked.
5. Ask for reasons from the majority group or allow them to state their case. You will probably not have to *ask* them. Strengthen their arguments if necessary by questions which open up new points in their favor.
6. Let nature take its course; let proponents of both sides continue the discussion, but break in when necessary with questions designed to strengthen whichever case seems to need it at that moment. *Do not reveal which side you favor by anything you say or do, or by your facial expression.*
7. When, and only when, both sides have had ample opportunity to defend their stands, and when you have made sure that all phases of the question have been explored, either allow the stronger side to convince the minority, or arrive at a satisfactory compromise. Generally, if there is a right answer or one conclusion which is markedly better, the group will arrive at it unaided.
8. If they do not, summarize the reasons pro and con, and try to get an agreement.

You must be sure to do two things to make this highly effective technique work for you:

1. Find out everyone's opinion first, before you allow anyone to give his reasons for his stand.
2. Keep both sides of the argument as equally balanced as long as you can by bringing out points they may have overlooked.

Suspense is one of the most potent methods of arousing and maintaining interest. Inviting competition is another. This procedure involves both of these strongly.

In finding out how everyone stands on the question, avoid if possible asking for a show of hands—a vote. Instead, pick out one person and ask him his opinion, cautioning him not to give his reasons—yet. Then simply ask how many agree and how many disagree. If they choose to indicate their agreement by raising their hands, all right, but don't ask them to do it.

Using a "problem check list." While generally a group meets to discuss a specific problem pretty well agreed upon beforehand, sometimes just a general topic is suggested, and it is the duty of the group to select the problem it wishes to discuss. In a situation of this kind, the response to the leader's question, "Well, just what problems do we want to discuss tonight?", might be just a little disappointing. No one, or very few, might have any bright ideas.

To avoid this, prepare a list of possible problems which you feel they might wish to discuss, have them duplicated or mimeographed so that there is a copy for everyone. See that each has a copy and ask that he check the one, two, or three which he would like to have discussed. After they have done this, take a poll and use the problem in which there was evidently the most interest. See page 37 for an example and additional uses of this technique.

Curbing the over-talkative person. He, of course, is just our old friend the "monopolizer" or Mr. Table-Thumper. Ignore him if you can; don't see or hear his efforts to get the floor; don't let him catch your eye. Instead, give your attention to anyone else who indicates a desire to speak. If he won't be ignored; if he gets wound up and well under way, your only recourse may be to forget that you're a gentleman or a lady and simply interrupt him, compliment him on his contribution, and ask someone else to take it from there.

Encouraging the shy person—Mr. Mute. One of your main jobs as a leader is to see that everyone takes part. You'll always have those who would rather listen than talk. Keep your eyes open for them and as you spot them, encourage them to take part. For example, when someone has made a statement, ask, "What do you think of that statement, Mr. Mute? Do you agree or disagree?" Or, "Do you have anything to add to that statement, Mr. Mute?"

Handling Mr. Sorehead, the argumentative guy. Refuse to be drawn into an argument with him. Make this a hard and fast rule and stick to it. Don't try to convince him. Your success won't be and isn't measured by your ability to get 100% agreement, so don't worry if one doesn't agree and aggressively says so. Ignore him and ease the tension with a joke or a statement (with a smile) that you're not going to try to convince him and argue with him. Generally the others will take care of him.

Bringing the group to a decision. Too many conference discussions don't seem to get anywhere. There is a good discussion of the problem, but no decisions reached. It is the duty of the leader, of course, to see that this doesn't happen. Here is where he must play the role of *summarizer* and help arrive at an agreement as to a solution or an answer to the problem under discussion. There are a number of ways in which this can be done. Sometimes all that will be necessary will be to do it on a "general consent" basis, saying, "Well, on the basis of what we've discussed it seems that most of us feel, etc., etc." Again, it may be necessary to restate the arguments for and against the proposal under consideration and call for a decision by the group, or suggest the decision.

One of the better ways, and a method which will lead and help the group to weigh the facts and arrive at their own conclusions is the one outlined below. It consists of the leader asking the group to apply a three-way test to each or all of the solutions suggested and on the basis of this test arrive at a conclusion. This test involves these questions to be asked by the leader as overhead questions.

1. Will this solution accomplish what we want to have happen? Will it attain our major purposes?
2. Can it be done? Is it feasible?
3. Do the facts justify it? What facts support it? Which are in conflict with it?

This test applied to each of the stands or solutions proposed by the group will generally indicate which is the best.

In summary, these things characterize a good discussion and effective democratic leadership:

1. It is informal. The leader establishes that kind of an atmosphere.
2. Everyone participates. The leader makes it a point to see that they do, and that he doesn't monopolize the discussion.
3. It maintains a cooperative attitude.
4. It stimulates thinking. The leader presents problem situations, brings out all pertinent facts, keeps the arguments balanced, and brings them to a definite conclusion.
5. It accomplishes something. Decisions are made.
6. The members are interested. The leader creates and maintains suspense, uses interesting procedures.
7. It checks up on itself. It makes use of either an official or unofficial observer.

CHAPTER VI

CONDUCTING FORMAL BUSINESS MEETINGS

The formal business meeting, conducted according to the rules of parliamentary procedure, has a very important place in our social order and way of life. In fact you are more likely to be called upon to lead a meeting of this kind than any of the other types we have described and discussed. While it differs from most of the other kinds of meetings in that it is more formal and conducted in accordance with rather strict parliamentary procedure, many of the same rules for effective leadership apply. There are, however, these differences, which affect your job as leader or presiding officer.

1. Tradition has defined a well established order of business which you would do well to know and to follow.

2. You have far more powers both expressed and implied than does the leader of a less formal discussion meeting.

3. The members of your group will be more or less familiar with the processes of parliamentary procedure and will be involuntarily checking up on your work as a leader.

4. Deliberations result generally in formal recorded action; formal proposals are made, discussed, voted upon, and recorded.

5. Deliberations themselves, as well as the order of business, follow recognized rules of procedure.

Your first responsibility as a leader or presiding officer of a group of this kind, then, is to become familiar with the rules of the game, with parliamentary procedure. It is not the purpose of this book to reproduce these rules nor to discuss them except incidentally. They may be found in many publications, but several of the simpler and better ones which are listed below may be obtained free or at little cost.

"The Meeting Will Come to Order" by Harold Sponberg is excellent. It is published by Michigan State University as Extension Bulletin 294, and may be obtained free or at a nominal cost from this institution at East Lansing.

"A Guide to Parliamentary Practices" by Melvin Henderson and Herbert J. Rucker published by The Interstate Printers & Publishers, Inc., 19-27 No. Jackson Street, Danville, Illinois, and "Helps In Mastering Parliamentary Procedure" by Wilbur F. Stewart, published by The Enterprise Cooperative Co., New Concord, Ohio, are both valuable handbooks which identify and discuss clearly and briefly the important rules of parliamentary procedure. The "Bible," of course, is Robert's "Rules of Order."

A little study of any of these will give you the know-how you need to go through the motions (no pun intended) of such a meeting. Knowing these rules, let us take a look at your job as a leader and what you should and may do to make such meetings run smoothly and function effectively.

Your major responsibilities as presiding officer of a formal meeting are these:

1. To *initiate* items or proposals for the members to consider; to bring before the group matters on which they may wish to take action.

2. To *facilitate* the deliberations and actions of the group; to make it easier for them to conduct the business which has brought them together.

3. To *orient* and guide the group in the conduct of their business.

4. To *encourage* and bring about a free and complete discussion of matters brought before the meeting. To act as a harmonizer when debate waxes a little too warm.

5. To *summarize,* clarify, and restate motions made and considered by the group prior to voting.

These you will recognize as leadership roles discussed in Chapter II, and emphasize the fact that the formal business meeting is also built around and utilizes the democratic process of group discussion.

Let us take these six responsibilities and discuss how you may discharge them in order that your meeting will function as it should.

1. *Initiate.* Bringing up matters to be considered in the meeting is a responsibility which you share with the other members of the group, but be prepared to do more than your share. This calls for a little preliminary planning on your part. It might be well for you to meet with the other officers as an executive committee, and especially with the secretary, to make preliminary plans for the meeting, anticipate items which may be brought up from the floor for action, go over the minutes of the previous meeting and see whether or not there is any unfinished business, and list items which the officers may wish to have considered. A brief meeting of this kind, the day before your larger group meets, will enable you to think through and prepare for at least some of the matters to be considered.

As you consider the order of business of a formal meeting, many other instances will be found where you as presiding officer initiate matters. The accepted order of business is as follows:

a. Call to order.
b. Reading of minutes of previous meeting.
c. Treasurer's report.
d. Introduction of guests.
e. Reports of standing committees.
f. Reports of special committees.
g. Old business.
h. New business.
i. Program.
j. Adjournment.

In taking care of almost every one of these items of business after calling the meeting to order, you initiate discussion or at least set the stage for questions and discussion. For example, let's assume you have called for reports of standing committees and the program committee has made its report. You, as chairman, might say, "Thank you. You have heard the report of this standing committee. Are there any questions about it? (Pause) If not what is your pleasure concerning it?"

Note that you have given your group an opportunity by means of the two questions you raised, to get to work. Twice you've tossed them the ball and given them a chance to take over.

So be prepared to initiate action by the members by such questions as:

"Is there any discussion?"

"Are there any questions?"

"Is there any unfinished business to come before us?"

"What is your pleasure concerning this report?"

2. *Facilitate.* This is your most important responsibility. Herb Caen, writing in the San Francisco Examiner, characterized a well-known entertainer in these words, "She is the kind who can make a 90-minute meeting seem to last a whole hour and a half." Formal business meetings are not too interesting to many members at best. Some of them may get a little impatient to get business out of the way and to the program and the eats. So it behooves you, as the presiding officer, to try to make that 90-minute business session seem, not like an hour and a half, but like only an hour. It can be done, too, if you do your part smoothly. Here's how.

Know your parliamentary procedure. Get one of those booklets we mentioned and study it so that you know the order of business and what you're supposed to do and say so well that it becomes second nature.

Use a parliamentarian. Even though you know your stuff, it's always well to have someone to refer the knotty questions to. Appoint a parliamentarian and have him or her on call with her book of rules to help you out of the tangles which can befall even an experienced presiding officer. *Keep things moving.* When you've given them a decent interval in which to respond after asking a question, pass on to the next order of business. Develop a sense of timing and use it. *Avoid making long explanations or speeches.* Your job isn't to give facts; it's to initiate and to facilitate. Above all, *don't take* the *chance* of *insulting their intelligence* by a *lengthy explanation* of something which may be and probably is just as well understood by them as by you. If you do have to play the role of fact giver, you should be the *last* source of information—literally and chronologically last. If you have something to say for or against a motion and feel strongly enough about it so that you *must* speak, ask the vice-president or some other member to take the chair and serve until the motion has been disposed of. Don't do it as presiding officer.

Use your secretary. Have him briefed to be ready with items of unfinished business from the minutes of the last meeting. Get him conditioned to getting the motions down on paper as they are made, and being able to read them off quickly and clearly when called upon to do so.

Know the patter. Formal parliamentary procedure has a language all its own. Study it; become familiar with it so that you don't have to hesitate, at least in handling the ordinary matters of business. At the end of this chapter are some phrases that should become second nature to you.

Keep your eyes open. Be alert and watch the members all the time. Don't keep your gaze fixed on any one person or portion of the room, and don't let your eyes stray to the ceiling or to the windows. Be on the lookout always for members wherever they may be who wish the floor, and be quick to recognize them.

Use the real authority and power that you have as presiding officer. Use it right, of course, but use it. No one can speak without recognition from you; you determine when to bring a matter to a vote; you decide and state whether a motion has passed or has been defeated. Don't hesitate, if you would keep things moving. That gavel was given you for a purpose.

Appreciate and use the procedure of handling business by general consent where appropriate. If a matter under discussion obviously has the unanimous approval of all the members, don't go through the process of asking for a motion, a second, and a vote, but bring the matter to a close by a statement such as this, "It seems to be the consensus that we do thus and so, and if there are no objections, it is so ordered." The approving of the minutes of the previous meeting, for example, is generally handled in this manner by general consent when the chairman states, "You have heard the minutes of the previous meeting. Are there any additions or corrections? (Pause) If not, they stand approved as read." Often the reports of standing committees may be handled in much the same manner. This technique is a most important time saver, so it would be well for you to be on the alert for situations where it may be applied.

The use of all of these procedures will do much to facilitate the conduct of business by the group. Study them and practice them. Maybe you won't be able to make a 90-minute meeting seem only an hour long, but at least it won't seem longer than an hour and a half.

3. *Orient and Guide.* The importance of your knowing the rules of the game has already been stressed. There are many pitfalls both for you and the group in formal parliamentary procedure. Strange and wonderful things can and often do happen in the conduct of even ordinary business. Just to illustrate, most motions require only a majority of the votes cast, but some require a two-thirds majority. Which ones are they? There is rank and order of precedence among motions. There are "privileged motions" at the top, "subsidiary motions" next in rank, "incidental motions," "renewal motions," and clear at the bottom "main motions." Which is which? How can the wording of a motion be changed without amending it, or withdrawing it and starting over? Suppose after a motion has been passed, you begin to wonder whether or not you've done the right thing, can it be reconsidered? How? Suppose someone makes a motion, someone else amends it, someone moves to amend the amendment? How long can this go on? How do you stop it? After you get it stopped, how do you vote on all these amend-

ments? Things can get mighty confusing both to you and your group.

Perhaps the best way to handle this is not to operate as a lone wolf, but to make full use of a leadership team—you as presiding officer, a good secretary to keep a written record of motions made and other important items, and a parliamentarian to get you out of tight corners. So if you would do a good job of guiding and orienting the group in its deliberations, get someone who already knows parliamentary procedure, furnish her with a copy of Robert's Rules, seat her right with the secretary where's she's readily available, and then let them try to tangle you up. You're ready for them!

4. *Encourage free discussion.* While it seems to be quite a common practice for a group to discuss a matter *before* a motion is made and seconded, this is not the correct procedure. A motion should be made and seconded in order to start discussion, and a member may make a motion or second it, not necessarily because he favors it, but because he wishes it discussed. Similarly you as chairman should, when someone begins to discuss a matter without it being brought on the floor as a motion, ask that it be stated in the form of a motion so that it may be discussed. Therefore, be ready with the question, "Do you wish to state that in the form of a motion, Mr. White?", or "Will you please put that in the form of a motion?" Then call for a second, and the matter is ready to be discussed. In conducting the discussion of a motion, make every effort to keep the discussion *balanced*. Give the person who made the motion the first chance to discuss it. Then try to get someone to present an opposite point of view to that of the first speaker. Alternating speakers for and against the motion will serve to bring out most of the facts which should be considered and make for sounder actions. Another good rule to follow is to make sure that every member has a chance to speak at least *once* on a motion before any member is permitted to speak *twice*.

If a really difficult problem is under consideration, make use of the buzz session as described in Chapter IV. Very

often persons who would be too timid to call for the floor
and speak on the proposition under discussion, will have no
inhibitions about discussing it freely in a small group. This
is a little used technique, but a good one where the group
is large, the problem requires free and complete discussion,
and where immediate action is preferable to referring the
problem to a committee.

To break up into buzz groups, simply ask for a motion
that "we discuss this problem informally in small groups";
have it seconded, discussed and brought to a vote. After a
specified time, each group is asked to give a report on their
conclusions, and the meeting resumes its identity as a formal
meeting. This device is not very well known, and as a result
little used. It is one of the best, however, in arriving at an
answer to a difficult situation which must or should be settled right now. It is surprising how an informal discussion
will bring out such worthwhile suggestions when the more
formal procedure of the larger group fails to do so. Try it
the next time your group has a problem of this kind.

The times when you as presiding officer may have to act
as a harmonizer are, fortunately, few and far between. However, when two or more members begin to get acrimonious,
tempers begin to flare, and tension to build up, be prepared
to step in and pour a little oil on the troubled waters. Your
own tact and common sense will have to tell you how and
when to do this.

5. *Summarize.* In the interest of keeping things moving
as well as taking effective action, you must be prepared to
summarize discussion and bring the group to a decision.
Sometimes action may be taken by general consent as described earlier in this chapter. In this case, you would simply
summarize the discussion briefly, state that it seems to be
agreed that certain action should be taken and that it is so
ordered. Before calling for a vote, you should restate the
motion or have the secretary read it if it is long and involved, ask "Are you ready for the question?", and then
put it to a vote.

These five sum up the roles you should play as presiding officer. Here is another skill that every group leader should have:

Getting Effective Committee Work

Much of the business of a formal group is done through committees. Therefore, upon the success of these committees and how well they function, may depend the success of the group. It seems to be in order to poke fun at committees and their ineffectiveness, but they can be made to work. Try these rules:

1. Appoint as members only those who have a real interest in the assignment of the committee. Don't overlook new members and those who haven't already served. They may surprise you.

2. Be sure they can and will work together as a team.

3. Outline carefully to the chairman (and to the members if possible) exactly what they are to do, and make sure it is understood.

4. Then let them know that the responsibility is completely theirs and let them take over. The surest way to break down the morale of a committee is to do part of their job for them, even to the extent of making suggestions as to how they should proceed. Make it *their* job and let them stand or fall on their results.

5. Check with the chairman, of course, and ask for reports of progress, but go that far and no further in trying to help them.

It is in the failure to do the things described in the last two paragraphs that most leaders fail in getting committees to function. Give them a job to do, be sure they understand it, be sure they know that they have complete responsibility, keep hands off.

Some Things You Should Know

1. A motion should be made and seconded before discussion starts.

2. You should state the motion after it has been made and seconded, and then start the discussion by asking, "Now is there any discussion?"

3. A nomination does not call for a second, therefore, do not ask for one.

4. Reports of committees may be "received" or "accepted" or "approved." A report that is received has been heard, but not necessarily approved by that group. The ordinary treasurer's report should be *received;* not accepted or approved. A report of the program committee outlining the programs for the next three meetings may be *accepted* if the group approves the programs lined up. Don't ask that reports be accepted or approved unless you really mean to bring them up for approval and adoption.

5. It is in order to ask chairmen of committees to prepare their reports in writing and to give a copy of them to the secretary to become a part of the minutes.

6. It is customary for the member presenting a committee report to move that it be received or accepted. If he does not, ask him if he wishes to do so.

7. There should be only one main motion considered at a time.

8. A main motion is one that brings an item of business before the group for action. It is the lowest ranking motion; also the most common.

9. A privileged motion is one that involves an immediate action of the group as a whole; that they recess, adjourn, etc. It is the top ranking motion and is not debatable.

10. A subsidiary motion is one to change, postpone, or dispose of a main motion. It ranks below a privileged and above a main motion.

11. An incidental motion pertains to the method of conducting business, e.g., point of order, method of voting. It must be disposed of before the motion out of which it came.

12. A motion may be changed without being formally amended by motion. This may be done by asking the maker of the motion to change his motion to include the suggested

change. If he agrees and no one else objects, the motion is thus changed informally.

13. If a motion to amend is made and seconded, it must be voted upon *before* a vote is taken on the motion to which it applies.

14. A motion to reconsider must be made by one who voted on the winning side when the original motion was carried.

What to say when you:

1. Call the meeting to order.
    "The meeting will please (now) come to order."
2. Have the minutes of the previous meeting read and approved.
    "Will the secretary please read the minutes of the previous meeting?"
    "Thank you. Are there any additions or corrections? (Pause) If not, they stand approved as read."
3. Call for reports of standing committees.
    "We shall now hear the reports of standing committees. Does the membership committee have a report to present?"
    "You have heard the report of the membership committee. Are there any questions? If not the report will be received as read."
4. Call for reports of special committees.
    "Are there any special committees prepared to report?" "Are there any questions concerning this report? If not, what is your pleasure concerning it?"
5. Consider old or unfinished business.
    "We shall now proceed to unfinished business. Madam Secretary, do we have any motions pending from the last meeting?"
6. Consider new business.
    "Since there is no further unfinished business, the chair will receive any new business. Mr. ...."
7. Handle a main motion.
    "You have heard the motion. Is there a second?"
    "It has been moved and seconded that we purchase a new rug for the recreation room. Is there any discussion?"

(Discussion)

"Are you ready for the question?"

"The question has been called. All those in favor of the motion as stated (repeat if necessary) say 'Aye'; those opposed 'No'. The motion is carried."

8. When a member rises to a point of order.

"State your point of order."

"Your point is well taken. The motion is out of order."

9. Adjourn the meeting.

"Since this completes the business of this meeting, the chair will receive (entertain) a motion that we adjourn. Mr. ...."

"It is moved and seconded that we adjourn. All those in favor of adjourning say 'aye'; those opposed 'no'; the motion is carried. The meeting stands adjourned."

10. *Always* speak of yourself and the other officers by title, not by name. "The chair will receive a motion. . . ."; "Does the vice-president wish to make a report?" "The secretary will please read the minutes." Thank the person who presents a committee report.

In Summary

You now have most of the common tools needed by the presiding officer. You know what to do and what to say. The rest of it, the skill of presiding, will come with practice. You will probably have plenty of opportunities. Use them. When you do, remember that even a formal business meeting is a democratic process; that it is your primary job as a leader to help this process function so that people making up the group can think through their problems, arrive at decisions, and take formal action in terms of these decisions.

A SUMMARY OF COMMON PARLIAMENTARY PROCEDURES

Acceptance of reports, minutes and treasurer's report. This is generally done by "general consent." The chairman asks if anyone objects and if no one does, general consent is considered to be given and reports are accepted. However, if one person objects, a motion must be made in order to dispose of the report.

Common terms. "Quorum"—The number of members present required in order to transact business legally. "Majority vote"—one more than half, ignoring blanks. "Two-thirds vote"—two-thirds of the votes cast. "Plurality" —more votes than any other candidate. This does not elect unless there is a special rule to that effect.

Common practices. In case of a tie vote, the chairman may vote, except on a secret ballot. He may vote to make a tie, but cannot vote twice. If one member doubts the decision of the chair on a *viva voce* vote, he may call for a "division of assembly (house)" and the chairman must take a mathematical count immediately. No second is required, and it may be called for at any time.

A *motion to adjourn* is in order at any time, providing its adoption would not dissolve the group. It must be seconded and is not debatable.

Only one *main motion* at a time may be brought before the assembly. It must be accepted or rejected before another motion is in order.

A motion may be *withdrawn* at any time prior to voting provided the chairman has not stated the motion. It is unnecessary for the second to be withdrawn.

Steps necessary to pass a motion.

1. The motion is made. Correct form is to say "I move . . ."

2. The motion is seconded. Member does not have to

obtain the floor and, except in large assemblies, it is not necessary to rise.

3. Debate and discussion.

4. Question. If no one asks, the chairman should ask the group if they are ready for the question.

5. Voting. The chairman should announce the decision on the vote immediately.

A main motion may be amended and the amendment may be amended *once*. These motions are voted upon beginning with the last amendment; then the first amendment, and finally the main motion as amended.

Nominations and elections. Elections are generally conducted under new business. Nominations do not require a second. A motion to close nominations is not in order until a reasonable time has elapsed. The chairman should rule nominations closed after members have had a reasonable time to make nominations. Nominations may be reopened by a majority vote.

Unusual motions (but frequently used)

1. Question of personal privilege. No second is required; privileged over all other motions except to adjourn or recess. May interrupt speech or any other procedure except voting.

2. To postpone indefinitely. Must be seconded; is debatable; cannot be amended or reconsidered.

3. Objection to consideration of question. No second required; not debatable; requires two-thirds majority. This motion is used to dispose of irrelevant motions or business.

4. Appeal decision of chair. Requires a second; can be made only when a ruling is made by the chair, but can interrupt a speech. It yields to privileged motions and motion to lay on the table.

5. Motion to reconsider. Requires a second; debatable or

not, dependent upon motion under consideration. Must be made by one who voted with prevailing side; can be made only on the day vote was taken or on succeeding day. Can be made while another question is pending even if another has the floor or after vote to adjourn, providing the chair has not declared the assembly adjourned.

6. Rise to point of order. A privileged motion which requires no second, and chair must make decision at once.

7. Previous question. A motion to stop debate, stated as "I move the previous question." A second is required; not debatable; requires a two-thirds majority. Affects only the *pending question,* so name is a misnomer.

8. Motion to lay on table. Used to postpone action; takes precedence over other subsidiary motions; second is required; not debatable.

TABLE AND RANK OF MOTIONS

MOTION	In order when another speaker has the floor	Requires a second	Debatable	Amendable	Vote Required
PRIVILEGED					
1. Fix time to adjourn or for next meeting	No	Yes	No	Yes	Maj.
2. Adjourn	No	Yes	No	No	Maj.
3. Take a recess	No	Yes	No	Yes	Maj.
4. Point of privilege	Yes	No	No	No	None
5. Call for the orders of the day	Yes	No	No	No	None
SUBSIDIARY					
6. Lay on the table	No	Yes	No	No	Maj.
7. Previous question (close debate)	No	Yes	No	No	Two-thirds
8. Limit-extend debate	No	Yes	No	Yes	Two-thirds
9. Postpone to a definite time	No	Yes	No	Yes	Maj.
(Special order)	No	Yes	Yes	Yes	Two-thirds
10. Refer to a committee	No	Yes	Yes	Yes	Maj.
11. Amendment to the main motion	No	Yes	Yes	Yes	Maj.
12. Postpone indefinitely	No	Yes	Yes	No	Maj.
INCIDENTAL					
A. Point of order	Yes	No	No	No	None
B. Appeal to the chair	Yes	Yes	Yes	No	Maj.
C. Parliamentary inquiry	Yes	No	No	No	None
D. Point of information	Yes	No	No	No	None
E. Division of Assembly	Yes	No	No	No	None
F. Close nominations	No	Yes	No	Yes	Two-thirds
G. Re-open nominations	No	Yes	No	Yes	Maj.
H. Method of voting	No	Yes	No	Yes	Maj.
I. Request to withdraw a motion	No	No	No	No	Maj.
J. Suspension of rules	No	Yes	No	No	Two-thirds
K. Objection to consideration of a question	Yes	No	No	No	Two-thirds
RENEWAL					
L. Reconsider	Yes	Yes	Yes	No	Maj.
M. Take from table	No	Yes	No	No	Maj.
N. Repeal or rescind	No	Yes	Yes	Yes	Two-thirds
O. Discharge a committee	No	Yes	Yes	Yes	Two-thirds

CHAPTER VII

PRESIDING AT SERVICE CLUB MEETINGS

B-o-n-g! You tap the bell on the table before you, the members of the club rise to sing our national anthem, and another club meeting gets under way. You've been elected by your fellow members as president of your service club. This is your year! One of your many duties will be to preside at the weekly meetings and to see that those meetings function as they should. Rotary International in its booklet, "Your Year," a handbook for club presidents has this to say about the importance of the weekly club meeting and your job as presiding officer:

"The weekly meeting of the Rotary Club is the most important factor in the furtherance of the Rotary program. You will, therefore, wish to devote considerable time and careful thought and attention, each week, to the preparation and conduct of this meeting.

"The weekly meeting offers you the greatest opportunity to make your personal contribution to the club. No other phase of your job as president is so exacting."

The same may be said of the job of presidents of the thousands of Kiwanis, Lions, Exchange, 20-30, and other similar clubs meeting weekly in practically every city and larger town across this and other countries. This is your meeting. You want it to succeed. What can you do to make it successful and interesting?

1. Have a plan and a time table for the meeting.
2. Operate as a team with your secretary, your tail twister or sergeant-at-arms, your song leader, and your program chairman.
3. Promote good fellowship by giving members a pattern to follow.

4. Keep things moving; don't let any phase drag.
5. Give them a "change of pace" from meeting to meeting.
6. Encourage member participation.
7. Know the objectives, functions, and policies of your club and conduct your meetings accordingly.
8. Be yourself.

Have a plan and a time table. While there may be variations in the general plans for meetings among the several service clubs and further minor differences due to local customs, most club meetings have three phases:

1. The *fellowship* period when members enjoy each other's company during the luncheon and talk over the affairs of the day.

2. The *President's time.*

3. The *address* or *feature* of the day's program.

Your plan should contain a time table and details of what will be involved in each of these three phases of the meeting. Kiwanis International in a booklet "How to Be a Successful Club President" by O. E. Peterson, International Secretary, suggests the following form for use by presiding officers in planning meeting agenda and making such a time table:

Time   Date_____
  Call to Order
      a. National Anthem
      b. Pledge to the Flag
      c. Invocation
  Meal Service
  Introduction of Visiting Kiwanians and Guests
  Announcements
  Club Singing
  Special Features
  Introduction of the Chairman of the Day
  Introduction of the Speaker
  Acknowledgment to Speaker
  Adjournment

Why not make the changes necessary to conform to the customs of your own club and have fifty or so of them mimeographed for your use during the coming year? Then, a day or two before each meeting, or whenever you get around to making your plans, all you'll have to do is reach into your desk drawer, pull out the form, pencil in details, and be set to go.

Operate as a team. Your secretary, your sergeant-at-arms or tail-twister, your music chairman, and your program chairman, are all a part of your leadership team. Use them. Most club secretaries, like Tennyson's brook seem to go on forever. As a result your secretary generally knows far more about the functioning of the club than you do at the beginning of your year as president, or at the end of it, for that matter. So use him. Don't do anything that you can get him to do.

Expect your team members to get to the meeting early. Be there early yourself. Eat with them before the rest arrive so you will all be free to attend to the affairs of the meeting. Show them your program and familiarize them with their parts in it. Then when you call upon them to function they will be ready and move into it without any delay or confusion. Encourage your music chairman to use some imagination in selecting the songs for the club members to sing. There *are* other songs than "Home on the Range" and "Let the Rest of the World Go By"! A good singing club is generally a good club. Impress that upon your chairman and song leader and get him to working with you. Many of these suggestions may sound trite. They probably are. However, these details, which may easily be overlooked, are mighty important to the smooth functioning of the club meeting. Once a circular from a western college of agriculture came to my desk. It was devoted to the vaccination of calves for blackleg and contained instructions for this treatment. The opening sentence was, "First catch your calf." Obvious, yes, but anyone who has tried to catch and subdue a vigorous, stubborn calf will testify that the author started with the most important step in this operation, trite or not.

Promote good fellowship by setting the pattern yourself.
Your attitude and what you do will generally set the tone for
the meeting. If you wish the members to greet guests and
visiting members and make them feel at home, set a pattern
for them. The fellowship period of a club meeting should
stress friendliness, the shaking of the hands of friends and
neighbors, joviality but not frivolity, the friendly mixing of
individuals and groups. That should be your attitude, too.

Perhaps the best suggestion is to be natural. Stuffiness,
painful dignity, and severity have no place in the art of
being a good presiding officer. Neither has facetiousness,
sarcasm, or a sense of self importance.

The tone of a meeting that is just right is difficult to describe. It is carefree, but not too riotous; it is friendly, but
not effusively so; there is fun, but not boisterousness; there
is seriousness, but not stuffiness. Perhaps it may best be
described as a blend of friendliness, humor, seriousness,
which produces an atmosphere in which business and professional people can relax, enjoy themselves, and still consider and promote activities which will make their communities better places in which to live.

Keep things moving. Of course, when you have a time
table to refer to, and when you have allotted a set amount of
time to each part of the program, this alone will help. However, much can and should be done to keep each part of the
meeting moving at a snappy pace. This does not imply that
any part of the program should be slighted or hurried
through, but it implies only that things should be kept moving. Think ahead. Know what you are going to say and do
next. Be brief and to the point in what you say. Be alert;
keep your mind on your job. Watch the reactions of the
group. You can tell from what they are doing whether you
are moving too fast or too slowly. If the attention begins to
wander, if they start looking at watches and whispering to
their neighbors, the chances are that things are beginning to
drag, so speed them up. If they act confused and don't seem
to follow what's happening, slow down a bit. Stick to your
time table and start and close on time. In an address entitled

"Twelve Ways to Wreck a Lions Club," presented at the 31st annual convention of Lions International, Honorable William B. McKesson emphasized:

"DON'T START MEETINGS ON TIME.

"After all, your club only meets every week, so give the fellows plenty of chance to get acquainted and bull around. The new members will be expecting you to call the meeting to order on time, but don't do it. If the clamor finally gets too loud and you actually have to start, always say, 'We're getting a late start today, fellows.' That'll call attention to your inefficiency, and after the members hear that every week for a few months they'll begin to come dragging in at any old time and nothing helps wreck a club any more than straggling membership.

"LET MEETINGS DRAG PAST THE REGULAR CLOSING TIME.

"If you're the kind of President who isn't interested in starting meeting on time, you'll easily take to this next suggestion, i.e., let meetings drag on and on past the regular closing time. Nobody likes to plan to do any other business after a Lions Club meeting, so no one is going to be anxious to get away. This business of closing promptly at 1:30 gets to be awfully routine. Some fellows are fanatics about it—you can find other things to be fanatical about. You know what a fanatic is, don't you? He's the guy that doubles his zeal even after he has lost his aim. You aim to wreck your club, so double your zeal about disregarding the closing hour, and you'll be surprised how soon it will be that you won't have any meeting to close. You're running a club—not a railroad—you don't have to be on time."

Give them a "change of pace." Nothing can be quite so deadly and uninteresting to members as to be able to predict, before the meeting even starts, just what will happen from the time the bell rings to start the meeting and when you tap it again to close it. Don't fall into the habit of doing the same thing in the same way and using the same patter meeting after meeting. A change of pace is just as important to a club president as it is to a big league pitcher. Get this fact over to your song leader and your program chairman. You don't *have* to sing the "Star Spangled Banner" to open every meeting. "America" is a good song, too. Some of the currently popular songs are just as singable as the old timers. It isn't mandatory that you have an outside speaker for every meeting. A good musical program once in awhile, a series of five-minute reports by members on their businesses or professions can well be substituted at times.

Vary your procedure in the introduction of guests and visiting members. It doesn't have to be done the same way all of the time. You can have each one introduce himself; you can introduce all of them; you can have each one introduced by the member sitting next to him; there are all kinds of variations you can use if you look for them.

Encourage your members as they visit other clubs to be on the lookout for novel procedures that they see on these visits and to report them to you. If they sound good, give them a try. It isn't necessary to change the overall accepted local pattern for the meeting, you can follow it and still get an interesting change of pace.

Encourage member participation. This is the keystone of every successful club and of interesting meetings. Sure, this is *your* year, but you're foolish to try to do everything yourself. Remember that participation begets interest, interest begets more participation, which begets more interest, and so on, like the Iowa farmer who raised more corn to feed more hogs to eat more corn.

Here are some of the things you may do to get member participation:

1. Use your board of directors. Assign them every responsibility consistent with their jobs. Make your board meetings real discussions, not the occasion for a personal monologue.

2. See that every member is on some committee. Set up the committees so that this can be done if at all possible.

3. Use your program chairman, your music chairman, your song leader, and your sergeant-at-arms. Give them a job to do and let them do it.

4. Get your program chairman to assign as many members as possible the responsibility for obtaining the program for at least one meeting during the year. Have him spread the participation of members out as far as he can.

5. Have one or two or more meetings during the year where a group discussion or a panel or a symposium replaces the speaker. Have the panel and the leader if possible selected from the members.

6. Use some of your own members as speakers. Let them talk about their jobs or their hobbies.

7. Stress group singing.

8. Assign members to introduce guests, speakers, visiting members. Train them or instruct them in making introductions. From the Kiwanis Club of San Luis Obispo, California, comes the card which is reproduced below. Why not have enough of these printed or mimeographed to distribute to each member. While these instructions are primarily for introducing a speaker, they apply equally well to the introduction of a guest.

"1. Take it easy; the audience is with you—it's the speaker who should worry.
2. Look, talk, feel happy.
3. Make it brief and enthusiastic.
4. Talk a bit faster than usual.
5. Talk louder than usual, unless there is a microphone.
6. If you can be really funny, O.K.; otherwise don't try.
7. Tell mostly personal things about the speaker, things that were not in advance publicity.
8. Speak as if talking to a friend. Don't memorize or read.
9. Save the speaker's name until the last, and make it forceful.

10. Start the applause as the speaker rises, and remain standing until speaker acknowledges his introduction.
11. Sit down, feeling pretty good about the job you have just done."

The way to get members to feel that this is their club and their meeting is to make it so. Get everyone into the act if you can, and see to it that they succeed.

Know the purposes, functions and policies of your club and conduct your meetings accordingly. Every organization, and every local club within each organization has certain policies and rules. In addition there are unwritten customs which are just as important if not more so than those in the books. Know these and follow them.

Get a complete file of the literature compiled and distributed by the executive secretary or the head office of your organization. Study it so that your program is in harmony with over-all policy. Much of this excellent material is designed primarily for club presidents. Rotary International has its "YOUR YEAR—A Practical Handbook for the Club President." Kiwanis International publishes "HOW TO BE A SUCCESSFUL CLUB PRESIDENT." Lions International distributes its "MONTHLY NEWSLETTER" prepared especially for Lions Club officers.

Know your organization, what it stands for, and how it operates. Nothing will add more to your feeling of security whether you are leading a board meeting or presiding at the weekly luncheon.

Be yourself. There is no one type of personality that you can identify as the ideal. So don't try to copy someone else. You are the right kind of a guy or you wouldn't have been elected to serve your organization. John got by on his sense of humor, on his ability to wisecrack, and his knack of telling funny stories so that they were really funny. Dick had a successful year because he always wore a smile, everyone liked him, and he just worked hard at his job. Chester couldn't see a joke even if someone drew him a picture of it. He was strictly business. He was a good club president because he *was* businesslike and sincere and the members knew it and respected him for it. Now what about you? What have you got? What are your assets? You must have some, so analyze them and use them to the best advantage. Don't try to copy John or Dick or Chester. Be yourself.

Being yourself will take you a big step toward being a good presiding officer. If you're just being you, you'll be at ease, you'll be natural, and your group will sense it and go along with you. There are just two habits that you should cultivate and develop if you haven't already done so.

1. Smile. This isn't an awfully serious business, after all.

2. Say "Thank you," and mean it.

This is *your year*.

CHAPTER VIII

CONDUCTING PANEL DISCUSSIONS

A panel discussion is a method of informing a group regarding a subject by giving them an opportunity to hear the subject discussed informally by a smaller group. This small group or panel is generally made up of people whose wider knowledge and experience with the subject under discussion enables them to discuss it with some authority. It may, however, be just a small group picked from a meeting too large for a round table discussion.

In reality it is an informal group or round table discussion held before an audience. Many so-called panels where several speakers present short talks are really symposiums. Handled correctly, the panel not only provides an audience an opportunity to listen to an informal discussion of a problem, but also to participate in some measure. Controversial issues lend themselves readily to this type of meeting, but other subjects may be discussed with equal effectiveness. Problems, however, and not topics should form the basis for the discussion by a panel.

The panel itself consists of from five to as many as eight or ten members and a discussion leader. They should be seated in a semi-circle facing the audience proper, with the leader either in the middle chair or at one end, preferably the latter. Don't line them up facing the audience; they should be talking primarily to each other not to the larger group. If a platform is available and sufficiently large to accommodate them, use it. If not, it is not a necessity that a stage or platform be used unless the size of the crowd so indicates.

There is a practical limitation to the size of the audience before which a panel may perform effectively. Since the

126

discussion is carried on in a conversational tone, the audience must be small enough and close enough to hear clearly. Perhaps 150-200 is the upper limit unless microphones are used by the panel.

Perhaps the best way to describe how panels are planned and conducted would be to describe an actual program.

In this case the audience was about a hundred high school and junior college teachers of farm mechanics—shop work. The subject, "What are the trends in farm mechanization, and what effect should these trends have on what we teach in our shops?" The general chairman of the meeting selected and invited the panel members and the leader by letter, informing them of the subject, the names of the participants, the date, place, and other pertinent information. There were seven panel members, two farmers who operated large, successful farms, two teachers of farm mechanics—one employed in a large high school, one in a junior college, two college instructors of agricultural engineering, a research specialist employed by a county school system.

Thus at least three points of view on this subject were provided for, that of the farmer, the teacher, the college professor. The research specialist was included because he had conducted a study of farms in the county and could provide pertinent facts. Thus he was cast in the role of fact-giver or resource person.

No further instructions other than the original letter and a copy of the over-all program of the meeting were given the panel members until they arrived at the meeting. There the leader met with them for perhaps five or ten minutes. He outlined his plan for the meeting. Briefed, it was this:

1. That he would ask two main questions:
    (a) What are the really significant things that are happening now in farm mechanization?
    (b) As a result of these changes, what changes should be made in the content of shop courses for farm boys?

2. That he would like to have them discuss these two questions informally; that no one would be expected to "make a speech."

3. That the two college instructors take notes on the discussion and act as summarizers—one on the first question; the other on the second.

These were the preliminary arrangements and planning by the chairman and the discussion leader.

An hour and a half was allotted on the program for the discussion. Panel members were seated in a semi-circle on a low platform with the leader at one end. The program chairman introduced the leader and the leader conducted the discussion as follows:

1. He acknowledged the introduction, stated the subject, and introduced the members of the panel. Rather, he had them introduce themselves by saying, "Your chairman has introduced me. Now I'm going to ask each member of the panel to stand, give his name, tell briefly what he does, what his job is, and why he feels competent to discuss these two questions. To start it off, I'll state my own qualifications. As the leader of a discussion, I do not need to know anything about the subject. I qualify fully in this regard. The gentlemen who *are* expected to know something about it will now introduce themselves, starting at the other end of the circle."

2. After the introduction, he stated the first question and let the panel discuss it for perhaps twenty minutes.

3. He then asked for contributions from the audience as to trends not mentioned by the panel.

4. He asked for the summary of the first part of the discussion to be given by one of the college instructors.

5. Following the summary he introduced the second question, which asked for changes indicated as a result of facts presented in the first part of the discussion.

6. After about forty minutes, the audience was invited to ask questions and take part in the discussion.

7. The other professor gave the final summary.

8. The leader closed the meeting by thanking the panel members and the audience for their contributions.

The elements which made this a success are evident and are basic to conducting effective panels:

1. The problem was an interesting one. It was meaningful and real to the audience. The fact that 30% of California's great cotton crop was being harvested by giant machines instead of by hundreds of workers painstakingly picking each fluffy ball might not capture the interest of many audiences, but for this one, it was vital.

The panel members were men who could speak with authority on the problem. They were known and respected. The two farmers respectively managed 10,800 and 3,600 acre farms. One employed a thousand year-round farm hands. They *knew* what was happening on farms.

3. They were conditioned to discussing the problem conversationally and informally. No one felt impelled to make a speech and no one did.

4. The audience did not merely listen. They knew they would have a chance to take part and did participate in the discussion.

5. The leader simplified his job by briefing the panel members and the audience as to the plan of the meeting and by arranging for panel members to summarize. This left him free to give his full attention to keeping the discussion rolling.

6. The discussion was planned. The plan was simple, but most good plans are. It was merely:

| The present situation; changes in farm mechanization. | ➤ | What it means to us. What we should do about it. |

This summarizes and illustrates the type of meeting where the *leader* formulates and states the problem to be discussed. Sometimes all that is given the leader is a subject or topic and he is expected to draw out the statement of the problem or problems from the group.

This may be done in at least two ways. One very effective way would be to use the buzz session technique described in Chapter IV. To do this, the leader would state the subject, divide the audience into buzz groups, ask each to decide on the most important problem or problems which they would like to have the panel discuss. As the representatives of each buzz group reports, have the problems recorded on a blackboard or wall chart. Then have either the panel or the audience decide upon the order in which they would like the problems discussed, and start your panel to work.

Another method would be to ask the panel members to state what *they* felt to be the most important problems suggested by this topic, have these recorded on the blackboard or chart, ask the audience to select the ones they want discussed and to add others, present these problems to the panel to discuss.

Both of these methods provide more audience participation than the first one described but take more time, so that there may be danger that at the end of the meeting a number of problems have been identified but precious few of them settled. All, however, are good procedures to be used as the situation dictates.

The Question Panel. In certain situations the "question panel" provides an interesting variation from the usual types of panel discussions and/or symposiums and promises to be a most effective method of presenting certain kinds of information in a way that appears to be most interesting to audiences. Essentially it consists of having four or five people on the platform, who, under the guidance of a leader or panel moderator, respond to questions from a similar number of questioners. After some time is given to the responses to questions raised by panelists on the platform, the meeting may be thrown open to further questions from the audience. Formal presentations by either the questioners or the respondents are eliminated by having the respondents, prior to the meeting, submit prepared statements which are duplicated and placed in the hands of the questioners and the audience sometime before the meeting itself. During the presentations therefore, the respondents are only called upon to defend or explain the position taken in the printed materials which are in the hands of the audience rather than to make formal presentations.

There are at least two kinds of subjects to which this kind of presentation seems to be exceptionally well adapted: those in which respondents who have each achieved some distinction by having done some phase of their work exceptionally well are asked to explain how they accomplished the results which they obtained, and those in which four or five people with different points of view on a specific subject have each made their positions clear in brief written presentations, and then defend and explain their points of view in response to questions from the panelists and from the audience.

In a most successful question panel in which the author participated recently, six teachers, each of whom had done an outstanding piece of work in six different types of situations were asked to submit briefs of their accomplishments. These were duplicated and distributed to the audience perhaps forty-five minutes to an hour prior to the time the panel was presented. The six questioners were supervisors and teacher educators who also had been furnished with copies of the materials prepared by the teachers several weeks before and so were able to prepare their questions well ahead of their appearance on the program. Questioners were briefed and told that their questions should be almost entirely designed to bring from the respondents answers to the question "How did you do it?" The respondents were also informed that their answers should be limited to explanations of how they had obtained the results for which they were distinguished.

The physical arrangements for a panel of this kind appear to be quite important. In this one the respondents were seated at a long table facing the audience, the questioners at two shorter tables sat at right angles to that at which the respondents were seated. The seating arrangement then was a rather shallow "U" with the opening facing the audience.

Since the panelists, both questioners and respondents, were accustomed to the more usual type of panel in which formal presentations were made, they expressed considerable concern prior to the meeting as to how well this would succeed and whether it would be possible to utilize the two hours allotted for this part of the program. The leader was besieged with questions such as, "Just what do I say?" "What do you expect me to do?" "Don't you want me to present a planned talk?" "How will we ever use all the time that is allotted to us?" They were assured that no formal presentations were necessary and that if there were no questions from the questioners or the audience, we would simply sit there and let nature take its course, winding up with the suggestion that they let the moderator worry about the success or failure of this venture. It happened in this situation that the questioners were quite effective, had prepared a number of pointed queries, and that the respondents were equally adept in answering their questions so that much more than the two hours allotted to this activity could well have been used. As a matter of fact, questioners in the audience as well as the regular panel questioners were still clamoring for the floor when the time allotted for this activity was gone.

Summarizing the points which appear to be key factors in the success of the question panel, the following seem to be those which would be most important:

1. Use this type of a presentation where you wish to have several people explain how they have accomplished a particular task successfully. Use it also where you wish to present several points of view or several positions on a specific topic and where you wish people who hold these points of view to have an opportunity to explain them and respond to questions about them. This device could well be used in controversial issues.

2. Select for respondents people who have done something noteworthy and something in which the audience is interested, or people of some prominence who are noted for a particular point of view on some controversial issue.

3. Get written statements of their accomplishments or points of view from each of the respondents well in advance of the meeting.

4. Brief these statements and duplicate enough copies of them prior to the meeting to provide one for each person in the audience.

5. Select questioners who are articulate, uninhibited and who have enough knowledge of the subject under discussion that they are able to ask and will ask intelligent questions.

6. Distribute the written briefs to the questioners some time prior to the meeting so they may have an opportunity to prepare questions.

7. Place the written briefs prepared by the respondents in the hands of the audience several hours before the meeting if possible so they may have an opportunity to read them over and become familiar with them.

8. Use one of the following platform arrangements: (1) either two tables in the form of a "V" with the moderator at the apex; with questioners seated on one side of the "V," respondents on the other and the open end of the "V" toward the audience or (2) one long table at which the moderator and the respondents are seated with two shorter tables for the questioners forming a shallow "U" with the opening of the "U" toward the audience. Naturally where the audience is quite large, it may be necessary to have microphones available for leader, questioners, and respondents, perhaps one microphone for each two participants other than the moderator.

9. The leader should introduce the members briefly. This can be done since written materials should carry the name, title, and address of each respondent.

10. In getting the questions started, ask each questioner in turn to direct one question to one of the respondents. After that the leader may well sit down and let nature take its course.

11. After perhaps forty-five minutes or so of questions from the panel questioners, allow a period for questions from the audience.

12. Finally the leader should summarize, either by making a summary of the discussion himself, asking one of the questioners to do so, or simply by asking questions from the entire membership of the panel which will lead them to summarize.

A panel of this kind avoids many of the criticisms which are directed towards the usual type of panel presentation. All too frequently the panel moderator feels impelled to give a more or less lengthy introduction to the subject, becomes entranced with his eloquence, and gives long introductions of the members of the panel. Also while the panelists themselves may have been carefully brief ahead of time to keep their formal presentations to a stated minimum length still it is difficult to control this matter with the result that too much of the time is spent in formal presentations. Again, usually the leader on such panels feels that it is necessary to rehearse and discuss the subject with the membership prior to the meeting itself with the result that the presentation may lack spontaneity. As a result, there is too little time for perhaps the most interesting phase of any panel presentation, and that is audience participation.

Although the question panel may not be a new type of presentation, the only one which the author has seen is the one described in this article. Therefore, it should be a novelty to the audience. In this panel, six respondents and six questioners were used. As a result of this rather limited experience, it is recommended that the number be cut down and that perhaps four respondents and four questioners would be a more appropriate number. From this panel and from other types of panels which have been observed, too frequently there are one or two of the panelists who are left out in any interaction and it would appear that four might serve equally well if not better than a larger number. This panel is essentially a variant of that which was used during the 1960 presidential campaign to present the so called Kennedy-Nixon debates in which there were two respondents, each of whom gave brief presentations, and then responded to questions from a panel of four, finally finishing with a summary in which each reacted to the position which the other one had taken. This type of panel provides for the maximum of interaction between panel and audience, and as such seems to hold considerable promise as a group activity, and as a variation of the usual type of panel.

In summary, the leader must do these things to make a panel discussion go:

Before the meeting.

1. Plan and think through the procedure to be followed. Prepare a clear, interesting statement of the problem or problems to be discussed.

2. Brief the panel members prior to the meeting as to what to expect.

3. Check the physical arrangements and see that they are conducive to effective panel participation and audience comfort.

4. Arrange for summarizers and recorders to assist you.

As the meeting begins and progresses.

1. Introduce the panel members.
2. Present the first problem.
3. Tell the audience how and when they will have a chance to participate.

4. Lead the discussion—keep it going.
5. Have it summarized when appropriate.
6. Present other problems as time permits.
7. Call for audience participation.

As it closes.

1. Call for or give a final brief summary.
2. Thank panel members and the audience for their contributions.

Note again how the four basic precepts of effective group leadership are applied; how the leader must:
1. Get the panel (and the audience) relaxed and taking part.
2. Become a member of the group.
3. Give them something to think about.
4. Help them help themselves.

The leader then, in reality, becomes a medium through which the panel and to some extent the audience thinks through a problem of some concern to them.

Avoid these things.

1. The limelight. Call attention to the contributions of others, not yours.
2. Set speeches or lengthy dissertations by anyone, and especially yourself.
3. Stuffiness and formality. Get your panel on a first name footing and keep it that way.
4. A dress rehearsal with panel members. A rehearsal is likely to kill the spontaneity that is wanted to make a panel really click.
5. Lots of problems, but no solutions. See that something is settled and accomplished. Don't forget the summaries.
6. Domination or monopolizing the stage by anyone. Keep *everyone* taking part.
7. Getting off the subject.
8. Wasting time and lengthy discussions. Keep it moving.

CHAPTER IX

CONDUCTING SYMPOSIUMS AND FORUMS

Symposiums are often confused with panel discussions, and many so-called panels are in reality symposiums. There is little real similarity between the two types of meetings however, and little reason for confusing them. Symposiums have more in common with forums. In the former there are several speakers delivering short talks on different aspects of a given subject; in the latter generally only one speaker. Their effectiveness depends largely on the amount of group participation generated by the set speeches and the methods used by the leader in stimulating the discussion which should follow the presentations.

Compared with the panel, the symposium is more formal and provides more direct information and instruction to the audience. It may be used before larger audiences than the panel, especially if there is a public address system available for the use of the leader and the several speakers.

If primary emphasis is placed upon the talks given by the members, the symposium as a democratic group process loses much of its effectiveness and is little better than a lecture. The only difference is that the audience has to listen to five or six speeches rather than just one. It, as well as the forum, however, can be a very effective instrument, especially with larger groups, for an interesting interchange of ideas and questions between audience and speakers, if handled correctly.

The key to a successful symposium lies in just three procedures:

1. Instruct the speakers to limit their formal talks to not more than ten minutes each and preferably five, and see that they do.

2. Instruct them also to attempt in these talks to raise questions about the subject rather than to try to give all the answers.

3. Use the buzz session with large audiences to provide well considered questions and contributions from the audience.

There are other techniques which will contribute to the general effectiveness of the meeting, but these three are the essentials. The following description of an actual meeting of this type will illustrate and outline the job of the leader or moderator of a symposium.

In this case, the speakers, six of them, were selected by the over-all chairman of the meeting and invited by letter to participate. Each was told in the original letter that he was invited to discuss the subject from the point of view of his own business or profession. One speaker was the vice-president of a large banking firm, one the executive secretary of an association made up of a number of firms and organizations, one the secretary of a marketing cooperative, one an income tax expert, two were college professors. All were well known, and well qualified to speak on the subject.

Following the receipt of their acceptances, the leader wrote each speaker allotting him a specific subject within the framework of the larger topic, requesting that his talk give an overview of his subject and raise questions in the minds of the audience, and requesting further that he plan his talk not to exceed *six* minutes.

On the day of the meeting, the leader met the speakers by arrangement at luncheon, and discussed with them the order in which they would speak, and the general plan of the meeting. The time table allowed approximately 45 minutes for the speakers to present their talks, and nearly *two hours* for the discussion to follow.

As an interesting sidelight, upon being informed of the length of time allotted to the discussion, one member, an experienced public speaker and a highly effective one, made a vigorous protest.

"You're away off the beam," he insisted, "no audience will ever ask that many questions. The thing will just die on its feet!" He refused to be convinced, but finally decided to go along with the plan.

An excellent job of expediting had been done as a part of the preliminary planning of this meeting, and some of the results of the good job of arranging are shown in the picture on page 140. Name plates were placed on the table before each speaker and a sheet of paper given to each member of the audience with the names of the speakers listed and space provided for writing down notes and questions. Furthermore, a timekeeper was seated in the front row with a device which featured a red light globe which lighted up when the six minutes allotted to each speaker had elapsed.

As the program started, the leader, after being introduced by the program chairman, stated the subject, introduced it very briefly, stressing that the audience was privileged to be in a position to benefit from the cumulative experience of the six speakers which amounted in total to more than two and a half centuries of know-how. He then briefed the audience on the buzz session procedure which would be employed, put them through one rehearsal, and introduced the first speaker.

At the conclusion of each speech, he thanked the speaker, led the applause, and signalled for the buzz session to begin. After about two minutes of buzzing, he called the crowd to order and introduced the next speaker.

After all the speakers were finished and the final buzz session concluded, the leader announced that he would receive one question only directed to the first speaker, and then one for each of the remaining speakers in order. After that, questions would be accepted to be answered by any speaker.

The results were most gratifying to the leader and the program chairman, and astounding, to say the least, to the speaker who had insisted that the audience wouldn't ask questions. In this particular case, the leader's problem was

Make sure you will have good questions from the symposium audience by breaking it up into buzz session groups.

not to pry questions out of the audience, but to select from the wildly waving hands, the one to present his question. At noon, the time indicated on the program for the meeting to close, the leader announced that time was up, but was over-ruled by the audience which voted by common consent to continue for half an hour longer.

Two secretaries, working in relays, took shorthand notes of the questions raised and the answers given, and the papers given the audience to use in writing down their questions were collected. From these a summary of the meeting was prepared.

The key again to successful symposiums: (1) speakers who know their subjects, (2) short talks which raise questions, (3) buzz sessions to give the audience a chance to formulate questions.

The same general principles apply to conducting a forum. Naturally, since there is but one speaker instead of six, his speech may be longer, but it should not attempt to give all of the answers, but instead point the way to interesting avenues for the audience to investigate and question.

Given an interesting subject, a speaker who plays his part well, it is, of course, possible to secure response from members of the audience without employing the buzz session. Too often, however, the results are pretty flat, and that dead silence that can and often does greet the leader when he asks, "And now are there any questions you would like to ask Mr. Smith?" is too embarrassing to all concerned to chance it, especially when you don't have to.

A question box is a fairly good substitute. In this procedure, each member of the audience is supplied with a piece of paper and instructed to write out a question or questions which he would like the speakers to answer. These are collected and read by the leader and answered by the speaker to whom it is addressed. It lacks the spontaneity and the interest of questions coming directly from the group and asked by the person who formulated or aided in formulating them, but it does ensure there being questions to answer.

Remember, the discussion is the thing in planning and conducting a symposium. The preliminary talks should be merely to set the stage, state and identify the problems, whet the appetites of the audience for the real meat of the program which comes after the set speeches are done. If this concept is held and rigidly followed in planning and conducting a symposium by all concerned, they can be highly effective and interesting. If not, well, you may have attended some of the other kind and know what happens.

CHAPTER X

PLANNING AND RUNNING CONFERENCES

Conferences have become an important part of the lives of business and professional people. Thousands of people in government, in education, in business, and in the professions spend countless hours each year planning for conferences, attending them, and running them. Most of you who are conference addicts either as leaders or as attenders are probably not too happy with what you get out of them. The story is told of one confirmed delegate who revealed his reaction as follows:

"The first thing I do," quoth this gentleman, "when I get to a conference, is to hunt up the registration desk and register. I do this in order to get a program. Then I take that program and go to my room. I sit down with that program and study it thoroughly and memorize just when each meeting is to be and where it is to be held. That's the best way I've found to make absolutely certain that I don't get caught in one of 'em. Before I learned this trick, I was apt to wind up in one or more meetings during the course of a day. Now I can avoid them and really enjoy a conference."

In most of the conferences of yesterday, and too many of them today, his rather unorthodox method of getting the most out of a conference is probably justified. If, as many people say, "you get more out of the bull sessions in the lobby and up in the hotel rooms between meetings than you do from the meetings themselves," that's not a very enthusiastic endorsement of the conference itself, or rather the planned part of it. While no one will deny the value of the fellowship, the renewing of old acquaintances, the making of new ones, the informal discussions, the bull sessions that are the inevitable by-products of any conference, why shouldn't the meetings themselves be planned so they're interesting and valuable too?

Conferences don't have to be painful either for the leaders or for the rest of us who take part in them. Conferences don't have to follow the time worn pattern that's all too familiar. They don't have to start out with a series of inspirational speeches by the "status givers," followed by a series of papers by lesser lights, each telling how he has solved some particular problem. They don't have to follow a strict agenda of speeches, papers, business meetings, and more speeches where all of the thinking, all of the business, and all of the discussing is done by a handful of people while the rest of us sit in patient boredom and listen. They don't have to be the kind where the only way to enjoy them is to make sure you don't find yourself in one of the meetings. There can be good conferences.

The Ear-Marks of a Good Conference

A good conference has these characteristics:

1. *It is a work conference.* The members or delegates do not come to be talked at, but to talk, to think, and to help arrive at decisions and policies.

2. It has for its purpose planned group action and real changes in attitudes.

3. It deals with *problems,* not abstract topics nor themes.

4. It is concerned with the problems of the *members* and not of the problems of leaders alone. It is democratic.

5. It has a definite action objective and moves steadily and inexorably toward the accomplishment of that objective.

6. It provides time for play and relaxation. The program is not too tight nor crammed too full of business.

7. It is constantly evaluating itself and the progress being made.

8. It spends little time on: (a) speeches of welcome, (b) introductions of people whom everyone knows or else does not care to know, (c) formal "papers," (d) speeches of any kind unless the speaker really has something worthwhile to

say on the problem under consideration, and can say it well. The so-called expert who "blows in, blows off, and blows out" has little place in a good conference.

9. It utilizes the latent leadership of its members and trains its own leaders. It utilizes as a team discussion leaders, recorders, observers, and fact-givers or consultants.

10. It provides a variety of meetings and group activities. It breaks down into small groups which work on phases of the conference problem or theme.

11. It doesn't peter out during the final day. It includes a final session that summarizes conclusions reached, and commits members to go home and do something about them.

Let's take a look at the program and the procedure of one that was successful and see whether there are some guideposts to running a good conference and for planning one. On page 153 is the program of a meeting. It was, as you will see, a three-day affair. Approximately one-hundred and twenty-five persons were in attendance. Some of the facts in the analysis to follow can be verified by referring to this program; others are not evident in the program itself. Let's start with the fact that this was a successful conference. Those in attendance all voted it to be one of the best they had ever attended. They agreed that it was well-planned, well-conducted, interesting to them, and yielded worthwhile results. If it was good, what made it so?

1. There were only four formal addresses, three in reality, for one was the summary of the meeting, and the speakers were tops.

2. Each of the formal speeches was followed either by a buzz session, or a panel, or both, so that the entire group had a chance immediately to talk over what was said in these speeches *in the meeting;* not out in the halls.

3. Every person in attendance had an active part in making the conference go. Everyone had a chance to say something; to discuss the two major problems of the conference. Many in addition took over other leadership roles.

Of the approximately 125 people there:

4 including the general chairman, made speeches.

6 acted as chairmen of general meetings and as panel discussion leaders.

21 served as members of panels.

34 acted as recorders: 10 for general meetings; 24 in twelve discussion groups.

12 acted as discussion leaders of smaller section meetings.

Thus a total of 77 people out of 125 attending took active leadership roles. In addition, all participated in buzz sessions, in the open discussions following the panels, and in four informal round-table discussions held in section meetings.

4. Everything that took place in the conference centered around *one problem*: "What are we going to do next year about building sound working relationships with the public?" There was one subsidiary problem, namely, "What do we need to know about our own work in order to tell others about it?"

5. For more than one-third of the time, the conference was broken up into six small work groups. Each of these work groups had about 20 members including a discussion leader and two recorders. Each group spent three and one-half hours discussing and thinking through some phase of the major problem of the conference. The conclusions reached were reported to the conference in general meeting.

6. There was a banquet, but no speeches. Instead, a good toastmaster M.C.'d a good program of entertainment. The crowd loved it! Only six people were introduced! That's some kind of a record in itself. The food was good.

7. There was time for business and for play. Meetings began at 9 a.m. and ended at 4:30 p.m.; at mid-morning and mid-afternoon fifteen minute intermissions provided a break. The only evening meeting was a banquet that was over by 9:30. The schedule was flexible enough so it could be maintained.

8. At the close of the conference everyone was invited, as a matter of fact, *requested* to pass judgment on how successful it was and to make suggestions for the next one using the form shown on page 156. In addition, one person was designated as an observer to drop into each of the six section meetings and take note of what progress was being made in each.

Now as to the planning:

1. At least three committees made up of from three to five persons each assisted the general chairman in the planning. This was not a one-man show.

2. The general theme and the major problem were decided upon a year in advance at a similar conference.

3. One committee planned and handled the physical arrangements, registration, rooms, etc. A second took care of the meals and entertainment. The third one planned the program.

4. All members were asked by letter at least two months in advance to suggest aspects of the major theme which they would like to have discussed and their suggestions were summarized and became problems for the discussion groups.

5. All discussion leaders, panel leaders, and recorders were called together for a preliminary meeting in which they were briefed on their functions and responsibilities. They went into the conference knowing what they were to do and why they were doing it. They were ready to function as a team to get things done.

Please do not infer that the way this conference was planned and conducted is the one and only pattern for a successful meeting. However, it is a good pattern and one that will fit a one-day, two-day, or a week-long session. There are, of course, other procedures which are widely used. Many conferences still are largely leader planned, leader dominated, and leader conducted where the membership and the delegates play a passive role. Trying to accomplish worthwhile goals in a meeting of this kind is like trying to get somewhere by driving on the wrong side of the street.

It can be done, but you'll leave a lot of disgruntled people in your wake and you won't be too happy yourself. The right-hand side of the street where people are going along with you is easier and more fun.

Therefore, if or when it becomes your responsibility to conduct or aid in conducting a conference, do these things:

1. *Make it a work conference.* Delegate duties, and involve as many as possible of those concerned in planning it and making it go. There is no reason why the conference leader should saddle himself with all of the thousand and one details involved in the planning, the preliminary arrangements, and the conference itself. Make it *their* conference, *our* conference, not yours. Get yourself a corps of assistants, brief them, discuss it with them, train them, if necessary, and then all work together to get the job done.

Three major committees, each headed up by one of your team, is about the minimum—one to handle physical arrangements: rooms, registration, reservations for delegates, printing the programs, etc.; one to take care of entertainment, banquets, tours, special events; and one in charge of planning the program and arranging for the speakers, discussion leaders, recorders, observers, panel, or symposium members, and other specialized personnel.

In the conference itself, involve everyone. In general sessions, use symposiums and panels instead of speeches whenever possible. Use buzz session in which all can take part. Break up the group into sections and, if necessary, break these up into other sections until you get groups small enough to participate in round table discussions. Make provisions for these sections to report back to the conference group as a whole.

2. *Start the planning a year ahead if possible.* Get your teams formed and working well ahead of time. Perhaps the last minute rush and bustle can't be entirely avoided, but it can at least be cut down to a bare minimum.

3. *Use a check sheet to systematize your planning and to insure attention to important details.* It is obvious that care-

ful pre-planning aids materially in the smooth running of any conference. The check sheet duplicated on pages 157-158 has been developed by the Public Service Office of the University of California at Davis and is used as a guide in the planning of conferences held at that institution. You will find that a similar one developed for your own needs will prove to be a most effective aid in making sure that arrangements are made for handling all of the numerous details connected with such a meeting.

4. *Go to the members to get the problems for consideration.* Have your program committee poll the members well in advance and find out what their problems are and which should be discussed. After a list of such problems has been secured, get a vote to decide on the one or two or three which should form the basis for the conference program. Let them decide and then carry out their wishes.

5. *Consider problems, not topics.* A topic or a theme is too abstract, too intangible to get your teeth into. Discussing a topic is like the report of the colored minister's sermon. A member of the congregation was asked what the minister had talked about the preceding Sunday.

"Sin," was the answer.

"What did he have to say about it?" inquired the questioner.

"He was agin it."

The objective of a conference should not be merely to talk about something, to be for it or "agin" it. Instead it should take the real problems confronting it and its members and try to work out solutions and plans of doing something about them. Therefore, in the planning of a conference, when the members are asked to make their suggestions regarding the program, ask for problems, not topics, and when they are asked to vote and decide, give them problems to select, not just general broad areas.

Here are some illustrations, taken again from the educational conference, used earlier in this chapter as an example of a work conference:

"How can we best explain that modern education does not neglect the 3 r's?"

"Where does vocational education fit into the secondary school program?"

"Are we giving too much attention to the education of exceptional children at the expense of regular pupils?"

"How can we fit organized athletics into the physical education program of the school?"

These can be discussed and answered. They are definite areas of trouble, of difficulty. They give rise to formulating plans for doing something about them, not just talking about them.

6. *Allow plenty of time for every scheduled activity.* The conference program that doesn't get behind schedule is a rarity. There always seems to be too many speakers, too many people to be introduced, too many unexpected delays for the time allowed. The result is hurry, confusion, hurt feelings, and not too much accomplished or settled. Provide plenty of time for everything. Make provisions for intermission, for 10 o'clock coffee, and for bull-sessions. Perhaps the safest rule would be to make up the schedule to allow about the amount of time you think would be about right, and then add about twenty-five per cent more time, or cut out about one-fourth of what you have scheduled. In any event, don't fill your program too full. Allow time for the unexpected.

7. *Have a few good speakers.* The words "few" and "good" are used advisedly, and should be underlined at least twice. Perhaps that statement is redundant, because there seem to be few really good speakers, on conference programs at least. A couple of drab, uninspired, and colorless speeches are all that is needed to ruin an otherwise good meeting. Better one really good talk than a half dozen mediocre ones. That's not an easy task for the program chairman to provide good speakers on every occasion, but it's worth trying.

After all, in a work conference not many speakers are needed or should be used. Those who are used, should be those who have something worthwhile to say and are able to say it well. Everyone enjoys a good speech, but it better be good regardless of the subject. It should go without saying that the traditional opening session of a conference with its speeches of welcome from the governor of the state (who doesn't show up but sends his third assistant), the mayor of the city, and the other Mr. Bigs, the introductions of distinguished visitors (all of whom are asked to say a word and respond with a fifteen minute speech) is not the most desirable, the most inspiring, or the most efficient way to start off a conference. If they can't be eliminated entirely, they should be cut to the bone.

8. *Use members as leaders.* Every conference group has a reservoir of latent talent. Use members as panel and discussion leaders, panel members, recorders, observers, consultants, or resource persons. It is not an impossible goal to attempt to have at least half of the members of a conference group taking definite assigned leadership roles in the program. Think what that means to the morale of this fifty per cent, and if these roles are given to different people each year, all can easily be involved over a short period of time.

9. *Make the final meeting a real climax.* The purposes of the final meeting should be at least two-fold. First to take a good look at what has been accomplished and wherein the conference has failed to live up to expectations; second to get public commitments as to what the members are going to do about the decisions made in the conference.

To accomplish the first of these purposes, the official observer of the conference may be asked to summarize what in his opinion has been accomplished and to point out the things which had been done well and not so well. In addition, each member should be given an opportunity to speak his piece and express his opinions on this point. This may best be done by passing out evaluation sheets similar to the one on page 156 and asking that members record their suggestions while these are fresh in their memories. These can later be summarized and made a part of the conference report.

If a conference is to be really worthwhile, it should result not only in some decisions made, but also in some action being taken by the members in line with these decisions. Now, how to get people to do this? Exhorting them to go home and do something about it is probably not the answer. Some means must be devised for each one to say what he is going to do and to say it right out in meeting where the rest can be witnesses. Then he's likely to carry out his plans. This can be done in larger meetings by asking for public statements from representatives of various groups. For example, in a national meeting representatives from each of several regions of the country might be asked for such commitments. In smaller groups, it would be time well spent to get statements from everyone, if possible or feasible.

Certainly this would be a far more inspiring wind-up to a conference than the typical last day with only a handful of diehards left listening listlessly to an endless list of committee reports, reports that are duly and often dully accepted with the full knowledge that little or nothing will ever be done about the carefully worded resolutions.

Far better some sincere statements in the words of the members as to just exactly what each is going to do during the coming year as a result of this meeting.

As said before, these procedures are not set forth as *the* pattern for a successful conference but only as one pattern. It seems certain, however, that just to the extent that the participants are purposefully involved in the planning, the leading, and the evaluating of a conference, to that extent the conference will have meaning and interest to them.

Department of Education
DIVISION OF INSTRUCTION
Annual Staff Conference
Sacramento
January 3, 4, and 5

Wednesday, January 3

8:30—Registration. Governor's Hall, California State Fair Grounds.

9:00—Opening General Session. Little Theater, Governor's Hall.

Chairman: George C. Mann, Chief, Bureau of Adult Education. Recorders: Ruth Edmands and George P. Couper.

1. Greetings to staff members, Jay D. Conner, Associate Superintendent, Division of Instruction.
2. Conference announcements and business.
3. Address: "Looking Ahead," Roy E. Simpson, State Superintendent of Public Instruction.
4. Buzz groups to select problems for discussion by panel.

10:30—Intermission.

10:45—Discussion by panel of problems raised by Dr. Simpson and suggested by buzz groups.

Panel Members:

Roy E. Simpson, State Superintendent of Public Instruction.

Jay D. Conner, Associate Superintendent, Division of Instruction.

Frank M. Wright, Associate Superintendent, Division of Public School Administration.

Herbert R. Stolz, Deputy Superintendent, Division of Special Schools and Services.

Aubrey A. Douglass, Associate Superintendent, Division of State Colleges and Teacher Education.

George E. Hogan, Deputy Superintendent, Division of Departmental Administration.

Discussion Leader: George C. Mann.

12:00—Luncheon. Governor's Hall.

1:45—Second General Session. Little Theater.

> Chairman: George W. Ormsby, Consultant in Audio-Visual Education. Recorders: Edgar B. Wicklander and Eli M. Bower.
>
> 1. Address: "Building Sound Working Relationships With Our Public," Frank O. McIntrye, Director of Public Relations, California Teachers Association, Southern Section.
> 2. Buzz groups to select problems for discussion by panel.

2:45—Intermission.

3:00—Discussion by panel of problems raised by buzz groups.

> Panel Members:

Carson Conrad	M. Eugene Mushlitz
Bernard Lonsdale	Mack Stoker
William H. McCreary	Nicholas E. Wyckoff

> Discussion Leader: George W. Ormsby.
>
> Concluding Statement: Frank O. McIntyre.

4:30—Tea Hour, Governor's Hall.

Thursday, January 4

9:00—Third General Session. Little Theater.

> Chairman: Samuel L. Fick, Chief, Bureau of Trade and Industrial Education.
>
> Recorders: Faith Smitter and Ralph G. Eckert.
>
> Theme: "Understanding the School Curriculum."
>
> Keynoter: Helen Cowan Wood, Assistant to the Superintendent.
>
> Panel Members: John B. Brinegar, Leo Jones, and Afton D. Nance.

10:15—Intermission.

10:30—Section Meetings.

12:00—Luncheon. Governor's Hall.

1:30—Section Meetings. Continuation of morning sections.

3:30—Intermission.

3:45—Fourth General Session. Little Theater.

> Chairman and Discussion Leader: Wesley P. Smith, Assistant Division Chief and State Director of Vocational Education.
>
> Recorders: Lillian B. Hill and Sidney E. McGaw.
>
> Panel Members: The panel will include one recorder from each of the six discussion sections.

4:40—Adjournment.

6:30—Division Banquet, Governor's Hall.

Friday, January 5

9:00—Fifth General Session, Little Theater.

> Chairman and Discussion Leader: Francis W. Doyle, Chief, Bureau of Special Education.
>
> Recorders: Beatrice S. Gore and Lee Bodkin.
>
> Theme: "Solving Problems of Staff Relationships and Operation."
>
> Panel Members: Helen Heffernan, Verne S. Landreth, Frank B. Lindsay, Gail E. Moore, Georgia Ruffcorn, and Stanley E. Sworder.

10:15—Intermission.

10:30—Section Meetings.

12:00—Luncheon, Governor's Hall.

1:30—Section Meetings. Continuation of morning sections.

3:00—Intermission.

3:15—Sixth General Session, Little Theater.

> Chairman: Donald E. Kitch, Chief, Bureau of Occupational Information and Guidance.
>
> Recorders: J. Everett Walker and Olen D. Davis.
>
> 1. Reports from Friday sections.
> 2. Address: "Major Goals of the Division," Jay D. Conner, Associate Superintendent, Division of Instruction.
> 3. Conference evaluation.

4:30—Adjournment.

Department of Education

DIVISION OF INSTRUCTION

Conference Evaluation Sheet

I. *General Sessions*

   1. Topics covered in general session presentation were:

      —Important and appropriate.

      —Fairly well selected but could have been more appropriate.

      —Not very well selected.

   2. On the whole the general session presentations were:

      —Rather poor.

      —Fairly good but might have been better.

      —Very well done.

   Comments and suggestions:

II. *Section Meetings*

   1. The section meetings in which I took part were:

      —Interesting and stimulating.

      —Only fairly satisfactory.

      —A waste of time.

   2. In my section the leadership was:

      —Poor.

      —Mediocre.

      —Very good.

   3. Members of my section:

      —Participated actively in the discussion.

      —Seem interested but didn't participate very well.

      —Showed little interest and participated poorly.

   Comments and suggestions:

III. *Next Year*

      —I think that we should have about the same type of staff conference again.

      —I would like to see us try a different type of conference.

   Suggestions as to topics or arrangements for next year:

CHECK SHEET FOR CONFERENCES AND MEETINGS
UNIVERSITY OF CALIFORNIA, DAVIS

(Please prepare in duplicate. Keep one copy, forward one copy to Public Service Office, Room 120, Library and Administration Building, phone 725)

—Make arrangements well in advance of conferences and meetings—

1. Name of Conference or Meeting _____

2. Person(s) responsible _____

3. Date(s) of Conference or Meeting _____

CHECK THESE

☐ a) Approval from Provost Office (phone 514)

☐ b) Check Housing Office (phone 535)
    Number of nights _____
    Number to house _____
      men _____
      women _____
    Time of arrival _____

☐ g) Parking facilities and street directional signs
    Police Department. (phone 712)

☐ h) Check Visual Aids needed:
    motion picture equipment
    slide projector
    screen – cord
    charts, etc.
    pointer

☐ c) Check Dining Hall (phone 586)

Number to feed _____

breakfast _____

lunch _____

dinner _____

Cost of meals _____

☐ d) Check meeting rooms, Registrar's Office
(phone 541)

Room preference _____

Time(s) needed _____

Permit issued _____

Report of Conference
forwarded _____

☐ e) Check printing or preparation of programs
with John McElroy, Agricultural Extension
Service (phone Oakland, Ashberry 3-4928)

☐ f) Check publicity for Conference, Public information, Davis Campus, (phone 597)

☐ i) Speakers aids:

rostrum, water

public address system

blackboard, chalk, eraser

☐ j) Publications needed—Public Service Office
(phone 725)

Manuals: manual number _____

number of copies _____

Bulletins: catalogue number _____

number of copies _____

Circulars: catalogue number _____

number of copies _____

Guides to Davis Campus:

number of copies _____

Career leaflets:

number of copies _____

☐ k) Miscellaneous:

posters _____

meeting people to be on
program _____

infirmary _____

CHAPTER XI

PLANNING AND CONDUCTING WORKSHOPS

The workshop is a meeting which has come to be identified primarily with education and educators. It is being used increasingly for the professional upgrading of teachers, supervisors, and administrators. Often it takes the form of a short, intensive training course in lieu of the traditional four to six weeks summer session or the longer, regular college quarter or semester. During the several days or even weeks devoted to it, experienced persons with common problems meet to discuss and to work out solutions to one or more of these problems, assisted by leadership teams drawn largely from the group itself. They learn together as a result of their own efforts.

It is a work session, and an entirely democratic process in which the members solve their own problems with a minimum of outside assistance. It differs from the discussion group mainly in the matter of size. The workshop is generally too large to function effectively as one group and breaks up into sections or committees in which phases of the larger problem are considered. It has many of the aspects of the conference, especially as to the number in attendance and general program. Ordinarily it differs in the number of problems discussed, in its objective, and in the fact that the conference makes more use of speakers and is usually more informative in its procedures. However, the more nearly the conference approaches the workshop in organization and procedures, the more effective it becomes.

There are doubtless many patterns for planning and conducting a successful workshop. However, it might be well to describe one which was quite successful, as it will illustrate methods which *will* work effectively.

The workshop which will be used as an illustration was one of three regional meetings, all of which were handled in much the same manner. It was sponsored by the United States Office of Education and held on the southern campus of the Utah State Agricultural College. It lasted five and one-half days, and fifty-eight persons were in attendance. All in attendance were either teachers responsible for the supervision of students assigned to them for apprentice teaching, or members of staffs of departments of education in colleges or in state service. Thus all came with common problems and with a fairly common background of experience and training in the field of the workshop.

Many persons participated in the planning which preceded it. A local faculty member acted as director and made arrangements for the meeting rooms, lodging, and meals for the members, registration, and printing the final report of the workshop. Supervisors and teacher trainers representing each of the six states participating recommended men to act as chairmen, recorders, consultants, and members for the several committees or sections. Furthermore, each supplied the director with a list of those who would be in attendance from each state. Each teacher was requested by letter to submit in writing prior to the workshop, a list of the most pressing problems he had encountered in his school plus an analysis of the facilities and provisions for supervised teaching which were available. Therefore, well before the workshop, the leader was able to set up his committee structure with competent leaders and interested members so that when the meeting itself opened there was little lost time or effort in getting under way.

The workshop had only two purposes and considered only two problems:

1. To formulate a comprehensive list of the essential training activities for student teachers in agriculture; to set standards as to the nature, scope, and sequence of these activities.

2. To analyze the conditions existing in the high school training centers represented and the problems which they

were facing, and to make recommendations as to their solution.

To this end six committees were set up; five to consider various phases of the first major problem and one to deal with the second. Each committee was composed of approximately nine persons, including a chairman, a recorder, and a consultant. Thus twenty-one of the fifty-eight persons in attendance assumed major leadership roles; two as director and leader of the workshop; six chairmen; six consultants, six recorders for the committees, and one recorder for the workshop as a whole. All the remaining members participated actively in the deliberations of the committees, the formulation of committee reports, and in the discussions in the general meetings.

The general, over-all plan of the meeting is shown in the tentative schedule which was set up.

Monday

    8:00- 9:00 Registration.
    9:00-10:30 General session. (Introductions, assignments to committees, room assignments.)
  10:30-12:00 Committee meetings.
    1:00- 4:30 Committee meetings.
    4:30- 6:00 Recreation.

Tuesday and Wednesday

    9:00- 9:30 Announcements, brief progress reports.
    9:30-12:00 Committee meetings.
    1:00- 3:00 Committee meetings.
    3:00- 4:30 Preliminary reports of committees.

Thursday

    9:00-12:00 Preliminary reports of committees.
    1:00- 4:30 Committee meetings to put reports in final form.

Friday

    9:00- 9:30 Announcements.
    9:30-11:00 Committee meetings.
  11:00-12:00 General session for consideration of final reports.
    1:00- 4:30 General session for consideration of final reports.

Saturday

> 9:00-11:00 General session for consideration of final reports.
> 11:00-12:00 General session for summary and evaluation.

You will notice from the schedule that the workshop program was composed of five major parts:

1. A general session for getting acquainted, presenting the problems to be considered, and the setting up of committees.

2. An extended period cf committee work.

3. General sessions for the consideration of preliminary reports of committees.

4. Further committee work to incorporate suggestions made by the group as a whole.

5. Final reports of committees and summary.

For the five and one-half day period of this meeting, some fifteen hours were spent in committee work and approximately the same amount of time in general sessions involving the entire group.

In the opening session, the leader of the workshop proceeded to get everyone acquainted by having leaders from the several states introduce the members from their respective states. He then presented the problems which would form the basis for the deliberations of the meeting, and made the committee assignments. The chairmen of the six committees were then asked to get their groups together in the room where the general meeting was being held and to get better acquainted with each other. Finally room assignments were made and the committees went to work.

Each committee was furnished with chart paper and crayon pencils and asked to submit both their preliminary and final reports in such form that they could be seen and read by the entire assembly. The general form which these reports should follow was agreed upon, but it was understood that originality was encouraged. As a result, a number of fine amateur artists and cartoonists were unearthed, and many of the charts presented in both the preliminary and final reports were strange and wonderful productions, with each committee trying to outdo the other.

While the committees were working the leader made the rounds, visiting each committee several times. These visits were made primarily to check on the progress each was making, and unless specifically asked to assist, the leader merely observed what was going on. Generally, however, there were questions asked about procedures or about the problem under consideration, and he participated briefly in the deliberations of practically every committee. As the time for preliminary reports approached, he asked about or noted the progress of each group in order to set up a schedule for the preliminary reports to the general assembly.

When preliminary reports were made, each committee chairman was asked to introduce the members of his group and to either present the report himself or delegate a member to do so. The buzz session was used in the consideration of each report and proved to be extremely effective. Since the reports were presented both visually and verbally, the wall charts on which the reports were recorded provided a reference for the buzz groups considering them. As the representatives of each of the buzz groups made suggestions and comments, the recorder of the committee reporting made notes of the suggestions agreed upon by the assembly in order that they might be incorporated in its final report.

While each committee was designated by number, the order in which reports were presented was determined by consulting with committee chairmen, and those completing their deliberations earlier were asked to present their reports first.

The schedule for this part of the workshop must be flexible to allow for the different rates of speed with which the several committees complete their assignments. In this case, it was necessary to deviate from the tentative schedule and to have the first two committees submit preliminary reports, then to return to committee meetings and then meet in general session to consider the other four preliminary presentations. Thus for a time, two committees were working on the final drafts of their recommendations while the remaining four were still preparing for their first drafts. This, however, is an improvement over the original plan as the committees which were still preparing for preliminary reports had the advantage of hearing how the first two reports were treated and could anticipate and correct obvious weaknesses before submitting them.

When the final reports were considered by the group as a whole, each was formally approved after being analyzed by buzz groups or if the report was obviously in good shape, by the assembly as a group.

As a finale, an evaluation session was held in which the workshop procedures and results were analyzed informally by the group and recommendations made as to the use which should be made of the conference report, plans for future workshop sessions, and plans for publishing the report.

In every phase of the meeting, an effort was made by the leader to expedite the proceedings so as to finish somewhat ahead of schedule, and the workshop closed early Saturday forenoon rather than at noon as the program indicated.

This was the program followed in a workshop which was successful. Both members and leaders were thoroughly well satisfied with the results and with the procedures. Therefore, let's analyze it, and draw out of it some "do's" and "don'ts."

1. It was planned cooperatively, and the planning started a year in advance of the meeting.

2. Every member who attended did some work and some planning before the workshop started.

3. The members of the group had common problems, interests, and experience backgrounds. The major problems of the workshop were their problems.

4. The workshop had only one major objective and only two problems were considered, each of which contributed to the attainment of that objective.

5. Everyone participated, and nearly half of those in attendance assumed major leadership roles.

6. There were no speakers and no formal speeches. Those present who had special knowledge and experience were utilized as consultants in the various committees.

7. Many group processes were utilized. Committees considered different phases of the major problems of the workshop; each committee operated with a leadership team of leader, recorder, and consultant; committee reports were presented visually and verbally; general sessions were conference discussions; there was a "get-acquainted" period early in the workshop; observers checked on the progress of committees; the buzz session was utilized in the consideration of reports; there was an evaluation at the close of the meeting.

8. It was an informal, work conference. Coats and neckties were taboo. State supervisors and professors were addressed as "Doc" or "Happy" or "Jack," not as "Doctor" or "Mister."

9. A healthy competition grew up among the several committees. Each committee soon became convinced that it had the best membership of all and outdid itself in dressing up and presenting its reports to the general assembly.

10. There was time for relaxation. All worked steadily from nine o'clock until four-thirty, and then played just as hard for the rest of their waking hours. There were no night sessions, other than around the card table. They took a mid-morning and a mid-afternoon break for coffee or cokes. It wasn't planned that way; it just happened. They worked all the better for it.

11. The leader presided at general sessions as a conference discussion leader, and acted as one of the observers. He didn't *direct* the workshop, but led it. He didn't *tell* committees when to report, he *asked* when they would be ready to report; he didn't direct how reports should be made; that was decided in assembly. He tried to make it *their* meeting; not his.

12. There was a change of pace. When committee work started to bog down and drag a bit, a short general assembly

was called; when committee reports began to get a little bore-some, further committee work was suggested.

13. Consultants did not dominate committee meetings. This started to happen. It generally does. A suggestion that they take it just a bit easier and let the rest of the members do most of the work took care of that reasonably well.

14. The meeting ended on a high note, it didn't just peter out. It closed a little ahead of the scheduled time. The final committee reports were not allowed to drag. They were not rushed through without full consideration, but the pace was stepped up. The finale was a brief evaluation session in which definite decisions were made as to what would happen as a result of the workshop, and plans set for future meetings.

In summary, it seems that a good workshop has many of the same features as the good present day conference. It is slightly less formal; it uses no speakers; there is generally no planned entertainment; there is a little more emphasis on work and the completion of a specific task; otherwise the pattern for a good conference resembles the pattern of a good workshop.

Therefore, if or when it becomes your responsibility to conduct a workshop, pay special attention to these things:

1. *Start planning well ahead of time* and involve as many of those concerned as possible.

2. *Make pre-workshop assignments* to members if at all possible, even though it may only involve gathering facts about their local situations.

3. *Hold the workshop where the members will be free from distractions and interruptions.*

4. *Give a high priority to having available the right kind of facilities.* A room large enough for a general assembly; enough committee rooms to take care of these smaller groups; secretarial help; blackboards or chart paper; eating and housing facilities.

5. *Use the specialists that you have as consultants, not as speakers.* A workshop isn't a course to be taught; it is an opportunity for the members to work out their own problems. Keep your consultants from doing the members' thinking for them.

6. *Keep it informal.*

7. *Highlight and emphasize the work of your committees.* See that their reports are carefully analyzed and considered, and not accepted perfunctorily.

8. *Keep it democratic.* Make it *their workshop.*

CHAPTER XII

CONDUCTING BUSINESS CONFERENCES AND STAFF MEETINGS

A business conference or a staff meeting is probably the most difficult kind of a meeting to conduct. Not only must the leader have and be able to use all of the skills of the successful discussion leader, but he must also be prepared to cope with some situations which are peculiar to these kinds of meetings alone.

Let's analyze these situations so that you can be prepared for them. First, and most important, to the members of your staff you're the boss, the chief. They, the members of the group, are under your supervision. In the ordinary course of the day's work, you're set apart from them. You are not really one of them regardless of how hard you try to be a good guy, to be friendly, to be democratic. You're different. You're the boss.

Next, they generally are not conditioned to accepting the entire responsibility for the department, organization, or agency as a whole. Each may accept responsibility for his own particular job, but generally he feels that the major headaches are yours. As a result it may be difficult to get them to think in terms of over-all policy and to tackle the problems which they may feel are the province of the "brass."

Also, they are more likely to be competitive rather than cooperative. They probably think in terms of "me" instead of "we." They may be accustomed to fighting for their places in the sun; for approval, promotions, for a more favorable budget in competition with other staff members or other departments within the organization. There are apt to be more cross currents and more suspicions. Since they may be meeting each other more often, perhaps in daily association, there are more opportunities for personal conflicts and differences to develop. As a result there may develop more clearly marked aggressive and dominative roles than we would find in other groups. We may find the attitude that "whatever that guy is for, I'm against."

Further, it may be found that more members of such a group will have a feeling of insecurity. Those in the lower rungs of the job ladder may not feel like speaking out and expressing themselves in the presence of their immediate superiors.

As a group they may be more blasé, a little more difficult to get fired up and interested than a lay group not associated together in a business organization. They may be more inclined to suspect *your* motives in asking their assistance in thinking through and solving problems, fearing that you may take their good ideas and the credit for them.

Therefore, in addition to the ordinary run of situations with which a discussion leader may have to cope, the leader of the staff conference must be alert to these attitudes and be prepared to deal with them.

Let's Take a Look at You

Do you have what it takes to do an effectual leadership job with your staff? How is that leadership expressed? Can you develop the habit and the techniques of really democratic leadership? There are at least three all too common types of leaders which can be found in almost any business or professional organization.

1. *The absolute dictator.* Generally he is a very able man. Perhaps he has built his business or his department up from a one-man show, where he *was* the entire staff. Since at one time he did everything himself, and made all the decisions, he finds it difficult if not impossible to delegate or to share these duties. As a result, he makes the decisions; nothing is done without his okay. He cracks the whip. He tells them. He rules. He sets policies and outlines the program of the

department. He emphasizes discipline. He builds a corps of "yes" men who do what they are told or else.

A friend of mine visited the office of one of these gentry recently and described an incident which illustrates all too well this concept of leadership. As my friend entered, the boss was just finishing the job of counting up yesterday's receipts. He stuffed the silver and currency into the canvas bag along with the deposit slip and pressed the buzzer for one of his assistants. As the man entered, Mr. "Big" handed him the bag, consulted his wrist watch and snapped, "Mr. Jones, it is now 10:15. Take this to the bank and deposit it. I'll expect you back here at exactly 10:30. That's all."

Now Mr. Jones wasn't the errand boy. He was a professional man, just a cut below the boss so far as position was concerned. Put yourself in Mr. Jones' shoes. What would be your reaction and your attitude? Yet many supervisors and administrators operate like Mr. Big.

For him, the step to democratic leadership is a long one, and the transition difficult, if not impossible. Worst of all, he may not see the advantage of the change. He gets results from his methods, at least as long as he is there to swing the big stick himself. While his staff may resent his high-handedness, they work for him. They may grumble, they may resent being ordered around, but they get their jobs done. They're afraid of the consequences if they don't. Can you imagine what his staff meetings might be like if he felt it necessary to hold any?

2. *The benevolent dictator.* He's a nice guy personally. In fact, he makes an effort to be a "good Joe." However, he still sets the standards, makes the decisions alone, and cultivates the dependence of his workers on himself. His staff members carry out his orders and his policies because they like him. He praises work well done and takes failure to carry out his wishes as a personal affront. He brags about "his gang" as one happy family, but when you discuss a problem with him, he does the discussing; you sit and listen.

One of my acquaintances falls into this category. Everyone likes him as a person, but when he presides at a meeting of his staff, it is a painful process for everyone. He seems absolutely incapable of getting or letting his associates discuss a problem and aid in solving it. His approach is to outline the problem, tell them how he thinks it should be handled, and then to ask what they think about it. His conferences are a succession of pleasant monologues and painful silences. The step to democratic leadership for him is a long one, too.

3. *The responsibility dodger*. He generally lacks confidence in himself and his ability to lead. As a result he lets his people do much as they please with little or no direction, and busies himself with details. He fails either to set policies or goals, and avoids making decisions until absolutely forced by circumstances to do so. He is the least effective of the three, for he goes to the other extreme. While he doesn't dictate, neither does he lead. Democratic leadership doesn't mean a lack of leadership, and the responsibility dodger may have even a more difficult task in changing over than do either of the dictator types.

The democratic leader. In contrast to these, the really effective leader and supervisor *shares* problems and decisions with his group. He tries to develop in his workers a sense of responsibility for the work of *their* department. He encourages suggestions and initiative in the development of new procedures. When he praises or criticizes, it is done in terms of the outcome of the work done and not made a personal matter.

Regardless of where you find yourself to be in this listing, you can, if you really want to, develop democratic leadership. The transition may be just a little more difficult for some than for others.

Conducting Staff Meetings

Now what does all this have to do with the conferences and meetings you have with the members of your staff? Well, unless you really believe and show by your words and actions that you believe that ten heads are better than one, even though that one be yours, better not try to hold staff meetings at all. A friend recently described a conference which was called to plan for a rather extensive and important meeting. It required that she and several others involved take time off from regular duties and travel quite a distance to attend. The leader was a pleasant, personable character, the kind you instinctively like. He was capable, too. They met at the appointed time. He opened the meeting and took over. "Now we'll hold the meeting at the Palace Hotel. We'll start it Monday at 8:30. Registration will be from 8:30 to 9:30. There should be a top-notch speaker to kick it off, and I think Mr. Dykes would be just the ticket. Don't you think that would be a good idea?"

A few dazed nods from the group, and on he went. He laid the whole detailed plan in their laps in about an hour and a half, asked them from time to time if they thought it okay, and at the end thanked them for their help and said so long.

As she left the meeting, my friend turned to the man next to her and asked, "Now just why do you suppose he asked *us* to come here?" "Darned if I know," was the reply.

Unless you can bring yourself to share decisions with your staff, to ask sometimes instead of telling all of the time, such meetings are doomed from the start.

It has been said that effective supervision lies in getting people to do what you want them to, when you want it done, and in the way you want it done, because they want to do it and because they have shared in deciding what, when, and how it is to be done. You may not accept this definition, but if you do, working with that staff of yours as a group, and getting them to work together as a group seems to be the logical way to apply it.

Therefore, to make your staff meetings what they should be, perfect yourself in the techniques of leading an informal group discussion as discussed in a previous chapter, and in addition put especial emphasis on the following:

1. *Plan a regular schedule of meetings and stick to it.* Prepare a calendar in cooperation with your staff; decide with them on the time, place, and length of such meetings, and then hold them as planned. Holding them when the occasion arises, or when you feel like it, just won't work. A hit or miss schedule results in far more misses than hits.

2. *Ask their help in planning the agenda.* Certainly you may have some problems that you want discussed, but so do they. Send a memo around well in advance of the meeting listing a few, but perhaps not all, of your problems and asking them to add their suggestions. From this, prepare the agenda and see that *their* problems get a prominent place.

After the first meeting where they have shared in the planning, get their help in selecting and assigning the duty of preparing the agenda to some member of the staff or to a committee.

3. *Share with the staff decisions as to the order of business.* Instead of bringing up for consideration first those things which you consider important, toss the ball to them. Say, "Here is the agenda which has been prepared. Now, what do you want to take up first?" You may or may not be surprised at what they consider important. Their ideas may be the same as yours; they may not. However, you've taken an important step in demonstrating that this is *their* meeting; *our* meeting; not yours alone. Of course, you can't afford to spend a lot of time wrangling on the order of business, but you can expedite that if necessary.

4. *Make sure this democratic process succeeds.* After all, one of your most important functions as supervisor or administrator is to see to it that policies which have been decided upon are carried out. It is extremely important that the earlier decisions made by the staff as a whole are adhered to; that policies set by the staff are enforced; that you show that you really mean to share responsibility with them. They'll be watching, and if you don't follow through on what they've decided, watch for storm signals! They have a right to expect you to do this. Don't disappoint them.

5. *Make the best use of each member's special abilities and talents.* Before long, you'll identify in your own staff, many, if not all, of the people you meet in meetings. You'll find initiators, recorders, expeditors, fact-givers, analyzers; yes, even blockers, play-boys, and monopolizers. Put their talents to work. After a time, if you find one or more members who have a flair for leading and stimulating discussion, have them take the chair. You may be in a better position to influence the thinking of the group, and to get your ideas across as a member than when you're saddled with the responsibility of acting as chairman. Don't worry about losing status. You have that by virtue of your position. When the discussion centers around some subject about which one of your team is a real expert, use him as a consultant—a fact-giver. Set him up at the head table and refer questions of fact to him. Use his know-how.

On one staff that it's been my privilege to meet with, there is a natural born analyzer. He is sharp. No one is better and quicker in sensing what is wrong with a proposal or a plan than this gentleman. He isn't so good at creating or initiating, but whenever a plan is brought up for discussion you can bank on him to ferret out immediately any weakness that it has. As such, he is a valuable asset to that staff; the very best kind of a balance wheel. His boss knows that, and uses him for just that purpose.

Identify your expeditors; assign them the job of seeing that the ash trays are clean, that the writing pads and pencils are set out, that the cokes are served when you take that five-minute break. In some organizations, the job of recorder is one that they "wish off" on some lowly member who can't defend himself, perhaps the newest or youngest member of the group. It's too important a job for that. Find out who gets a kick out of keeping and getting out the notes on the meeting and give him or her that job. When you give a person something to do that he can do well, you've got a person who is interested, satisfied, and secure. Furthermore, he'll thank you for the assignment.

6. *Make effective use of committees.* If the staff is large enough to warrant it, the use of committees will add to its efficiency. Just when "large enough" is reached is a matter of judgment, but in a group numbering twelve or more certainly some items can be better handled by committees more efficiently than by taking the time of the entire group. If committees are set up, see to it that their assignments and their responsibilities are very carefully defined, and that they are given time to work on their assignments. Make sure, also, that the people appointed to a given committee have a real interest in the work of that committee.

It seems to be the clever thing nowadays to poke fun at committees. Nevertheless, they can be made to work effectively. Two things to guard against: (1) putting the same person on too many committees, and (2) appointing a new committee every time the staff meets a new problem. Spread out the assignments; have a few good committees made up of people who are interested in the work of the committee to which they are appointed; define their responsibilities.

7. *Hand out more bouquets than you do brick bats.* There is an old, old saying that "you catch more flies with molasses than you do with vinegar." Don't be afraid to praise good work and effective contributions made by your staff members. Give credit when it is merited. Too often the quickest way to slow a man down is to bawl him out; especially in front of his associates. So look for and don't overlook opportunities to say, "well done." Just be sure that the praise is merited; that you can sincerely commend him, and that you don't always hand out the bouquets to the same person or small clique.

8. *Keep the thinking of your staff focused on improvements* which can be made in the organization. For some unknown reason it is far easier for many people to see what is wrong with a plan or policy than to sense what is *right* with it. Phrase problems so that they think constructively rather than destructively; so that they can look for improvements rather than criticisms.

9. *Learn how to sell your ideas to your staff.* Being a democratic leader and sharing responsibility with your staff doesn't mean that you relinquish your leadership. You will and should have ideas and plans of your own that you want to get across. Out of the many failures and the few successes that have been my lot in selling ideas to conference groups, and from observing people who do get their ideas across, this procedure has been developed:

(1) Get the facts and give the facts when making your pitch. If you really have the facts to back up your proposition, the chances are they'll buy it.

(2) Have an objective that is unassailable; one that they will all agree with and accept. Show how your plan will accomplish that objective.

(3) Present both sides, and don't try to hide or gloss over weaknesses in your proposal. It makes your case far stronger if you recognize and present the holes in your argument than if the opposition brings them out. There is seldom a perfect plan, so beat them to the punch and acknowledge whatever weaknesses you can see in your proposition.

(4) Present the arguments against your proposition first; then finish with the arguments and the facts which support it. In that way you'll wind up and leave with them a clear picture of the pro side and a relatively fuzzy one of the arguments against it. That sounds worse than it really is. This isn't trickery; it is merely emphasizing the arguments for your plan by stating them at the close of your presentation.

10. *Encourage and insist on straight thinking.* Get into the habit yourself and get the habit established in your staff of applying the following test to each proposal considered and to each conclusion reached:

(a) *Can it be done?* Is it in line with over-all company policy, or is it entirely out of line and utterly impossible?

(b) *Will it accomplish what we want?* Does it make for improvement? Is it fair? Will it build good will?

(c) *Do the facts justify it?*

When the decisions made by your staff are subjected to and pass this test, you'll know they are right.

In summary then, effective staff meetings are the product of three things:

1. The will and the habit on your part to give democratic leadership a chance to work.

2. Your ability to perfect yourself in the general techniques of effective conference leading.

3. Your use of the methods which apply specifically to business conferences and staff meetings.

IN SUMMARY

This book has been written for all persons who find themselves in leadership positions, either by choice or by virtue of the kind of work which they do. It is hoped that in the foregoing chapters you may have found suggestions which have been of aid to you in your own leadership role.

To paraphrase the final statement in the PREFACE: It has been written to you and for you. If it has helped you, if it has hit the mark more often than it has missed it, it will have been time and effort well spent. May it continue to help you when you preside.

Index

Aggressor, the, 14
Analyzer, the, 10

Blocker, the, 16
Brainstorming sessions, 44-50
Business conferences
  conducting, 168-177
  description, 81, 168
  types of leaders, 169
Buzz session, 26-31
  how and where to use, 28-31
  other specialized uses, 30
  use in formal meetings, 107
  use in symposiums, 139

Committees, 88, 109
  effective committee work,
    109, 175
Compromiser, the, 13
Conferences
  described, 86, 143
  earmarks of a good
    conference, 144
  evaluation sheet, example, 156
  planning and running, 147
  programs for, 153
Consultants, 18
  duties of, 91
  use of, 18, 165, 166

Discussions, group
  earmarks of good, 89
  leading, 87-100
  (see Round-table discussions)
Duties of group members, 91

Encourager, the, 8
Evaluator, the, 10
Expeditor, the, 11
Explanations, how to make, 68

Facilitator, the, 8
Fact-giver, the, 12
Fact-seeker, the, 12
Formal business meetings
  accepted order of business, 103
  conducting, 101-116
  described, 82, 101
  responsibilities of presiding
    officer, 102
Forums, 141

Getting members acquainted,
  21-25
  general rules for, 23
  methods of, 23-25
Group leadership, 2
  keys to, 2, 3, 4
Group thinking
  common errors in, 42
  importance of, 4
  leading, 40-43
  steps in, 40

Hall, D. M., 6, 14
Harmonizer, the, 9
Henderson, Melvin, 102

Informal discussion groups, 79
Initiator, the, 7
Interest, 50
  techniques to arouse and
    control, 51-58

Kiwanis International,
  117, 118, 123

Leader, duties of in group
  discussions, 92
Leaders, types of, 169
Leadership roles in groups, 6-17
  autocratic, 14-17
  democratic, 6-13
Leadership skills, 19, 20
Leadership teams, 18
Lions International, 117, 121, 123

Mallory, Dr. Benjamin E., 79
Meetings, kinds of, 79-86
  business conference, 81
  conferences, 86
  formal business meetings, 82
  forums, 85
  panels, 85
  round table, 79
  symposiums, 85
  workshops, 82
Member participation
  importance of, 3
Members, duties of in discussion
  groups, 91
Monopolizer, the, 15
Moreno, J. L., 37

Motions, rank of, 116

Observer, the, 18, 90
  duties of, 90
Orientor, the, 7

Panels and panel discussions
  conducting, 126-136
  described, 85, 127
  effective procedures, 129
  planning for, 126
Parliamentarian, 104
Parliamentary Procedures, 113
Playboy, the, 14
Problem check list, 36
  how to use, 36
Problems, 32
  defined, 32
  methods of presenting, 32
  steps in solving, 34
Proposals for change, 73

Question box, use of, 141
Question Panel, 130

Recognition-seeker, the, 15
Recorder, the, 9, 18
  duties of, 90
Resource-person, 18
Robert's "Rules of Order," 102
Role-playing, 37-40
Roles, group leadership, 6-17
Rotary International, 117-124
Round-table discussions, 87
  characteristics of, 89, 100
  duties of leaders and
    members, 90
  leading, 87-100
  preparing for, 92
  special devices for leaders, 93
  starting, 92
Rucker, H. J., 102

Secretary (see Recorder), 105
Selling your ideas, 176

Service club meetings, 117-125
  getting member participation,
    122
  plan and timetable for, 114
  rules for successful meetings,
    117
Six by sixes (see Buzz session),
  31
Speakers, 59-67
  arranging for, 60
  introducing, 61-67
  using, 67
Sponberg, Harold, 102
Staff meetings
  conducting, 171-176
  described, 168
Status-giver, the, 13
Stewart, W. F., 102
Summarizer, the, 10
Symposiums, 85
  conducting, 137-142
  described, 85, 137
  effective procedures for,
    137, 138

Testing proposals, 176
Thinking, group
  common errors in, 42
  leading, 40-43
  steps in, 42
20-30 clubs, 117

Whisperer, the, 17
Wool-gatherer, the, 16
Workshops
  conducting, rules for, 166
  described, 82, 159
  elements of successful
    programs, 164
  planning and conducting,
    159-167

Zipper-mouth, Mr., 17